The Perfect Consultant

The Perfect Consultant

ALL YOU NEED

TO GET IT RIGHT

FIRST TIME

MAX EGGERT and
ELAINE VAN DER ZEIL

ARROW
BUSINESS BOOKS

ABOUT THE AUTHORS

Max A. Eggert B.Sc., M.A., AKC, FIPM, C.Psychol., C.M.A.HRI

Max Eggert first read Theology before transferring to Psychology and then on to Industrial Relations.

He is managing partner of Transcareer, an international consultancy dedicated to Human Resource Management and Outplacement. Many thousands of people at all levels have benefited through Max's work and he has set many on the road to successful and profitable careers in consultancy. Max, who works in the UK and internationally, is a strategist, advisor, presenter and counsellor. He has two children and lives in Gateshead and London. His current passion is riding his cob, and his current interest is clinical hypnosis for career development.

Elaine van der Zeil, B.Sc(Econ), FIPD, MISMA

Elaine van der Zeil has gained experience in a wide range of Human Resource Management functions, principally in the Electricity Supply Industry. During her career in industry, a number of management consultants promised to make her life easier. Some did and some didn't. She soon got better at spotting which was which. Writing this book is her way of reminding herself what it is like at the receiving end. She is now a freelance consultant and trainer operating under the general umbrella of 'Developing People at Work', providing career and workplace counselling, stress management training and coaching in HR skills. She also writes business and publicity literature to promote client companies and communicate their policies and goals.

The Perfect Consultant

ALL YOU NEED
TO GET IT RIGHT
FIRST TIME

MAX EGGERT and
ELAINE VAN DER ZEIL

ARROW
BUSINESS BOOKS

Published by Arrow Books in 1995

1 3 5 7 9 10 8 6 4 2

© Max Eggert and Elaine van der Zeil 1995

Max Eggert and Elaine van der Zeil have asserted their rights
under the Copyright, Designs and Patents Act, 1988 to be
identified as the authors of this work.

First published by
Arrow Books Limited
20 Vauxhall Bridge Road, London SW1V 2SA

Random House Australia (Pty) Limited
20 Alfred Street, Milsons Point, Sydney
New South Wales 2061, Australia

Random House New Zealand Limited
18 Poland Road, Glenfield
Auckland 10, New Zealand

Random House South Africa (Pty) Limited
PO Box 337, Bergvlei, South Africa

Papers used by Random House UK Limited are natural, recyclable
products made from wood grown in sustainable forests. The
manufacturing processes conform to the environmental regulations
of the country of origin.

Random House UK Limited Reg. No. 954009

Set in Bembo by
SX Composing Ltd, Rayleigh, Essex
Printed and bound in Great Britain by
Cox and Wyman Ltd, Reading, Berks

ISBN 0 09 955601 4

British Library Cataloguing in Publication Data
A catalogue record for this book is available from
the British Library

Max dedicates his work to the late Robin Wayman, Personnel Director for the Parker Pen Company who believed in him when he and so many others had so little faith.

Elaine dedicates her work to her husband Pete.

Further dedications go, of course, to all our past and current clients who have shown such impeccable taste in their choice of consultants.

Thanks too to Ros Tovey who not only typed the manuscript, but co-ordinated the work as it came from London, Manchester, Gateshead and Sydney.

Thanks to Suzette Barker and Suzanne Gundry for the graphics.

ABOUT THE AUTHORS

Max A. Eggert B.Sc., M.A., AKC, FIPM, C.Psychol., C.M.A.HRI

Max Eggert first read Theology before transferring to Psychology and then on to Industrial Relations.

He is managing partner of Transcareer, an international consultancy dedicated to Human Resource Management and Outplacement. Many thousands of people at all levels have benefited through Max's work and he has set many on the road to successful and profitable careers in consultancy. Max, who works in the UK and internationally, is a strategist, advisor, presenter and counsellor. He has two children and lives in Gateshead and London. His current passion is riding his cob, and his current interest is clinical hypnosis for career development.

Elaine van der Zeil, B.Sc(Econ), FIPD, MISMA

Elaine van der Zeil has gained experience in a wide range of Human Resource Management functions, principally in the Electricity Supply Industry. During her career in industry, a number of management consultants promised to make her life easier. Some did and some didn't. She soon got better at spotting which was which. Writing this book is her way of reminding herself what it is like at the receiving end. She is now a freelance consultant and trainer operating under the general umbrella of 'Developing People at Work', providing career and workplace counselling, stress management training and coaching in HR skills. She also writes business and publicity literature to promote client companies and communicate their policies and goals.

Married, with three pampered cats, Elaine lives in Cheshire, is passionate about animal welfare and loves to sing.

CONTENTS

ACKNOWLEDGEMENTS

Our thanks to those colleagues who have shared their wisdom and experience with us, in particular Tony Berry, Tony Foulds, Lesley Gosling, Chris Pike and Michael Stewart, and to those other consultants from whom we have stolen so much, in particular Dave Parish, Fokkina McDonnell, Jenny Heather, Susan Williams, Neil Killian and Kathy Turner.

INTRODUCTION

We both specialize in the area of Management and Human Resource Consultancy, so the book is slanted towards that field. However, we are confident that our message will help anyone setting up in consultancy, whether in Marketing, Finance, Research, Administration, Import/Export or any of the numerous other areas of business development for the successful consultant.

Throughout the book we use stories, anecdotes and pieces of personal experience to help illustrate our points. To keep things simple, we do not identify the speaker each time.

The use of gender pronouns (he/she) cannot be avoided, though they are interchangeable in all cases.

WHY BECOME A CONSULTANT?

PUSHED OR PULLED BUT BURNING WITH DESIRE

Very few people wake up one morning and decide that they want to be a consultant. Embryo consultants are usually pushed or pulled into their new career rather than taking it up by choice. Most of us are pushed because we were fired. Some of us were made redundant and felt we did not want to commit ourselves to another employer. Others are pulled by the desire to do something for oneself.

Whichever way, it will still take more than being pushed or pulled to be successful; there has to be a burning desire, commitment and a strong need to make a personal contribution. In our experience it is harder to be a consultant than it is to be an employee. Consultancy is not the easier option, not so much because of the work but because of the competition and the way the market works, especially in the early days when you are setting up. So whilst recognizing that the best counsel is non-directive we must be very direct and say to you that unless you are steamed up on commitment then don't become a consultant because you just won't make it.

The desire needs to burn bright to keep you going. As executives most of us are used to working in teams, having great support systems and all the resources needed to do a good job. When I started in consultancy I had 'Me, myself and I' as the team and at times each of us worked a 40-hour week just to get ourselves established.

Still, as Paul Getty said, 'If you want to prosper, really

prosper, work for yourself.' Once you are on your way you will wish that you were pushed or pulled earlier.

THE GREY FACTOR

In an ageist world it is encouraging to know that in consultancy being the wrong side of 40 is the right side for the profession. Maybe it is something to do with our early education, but we expect to learn from those older than ourselves. Computing, high tech and PR consultancy are the exceptions to the rule, but by and large maturity is an advantage. Most consultants are bought for their experience and somehow that is not found on young shoulders. The university of life usually reaches places other more academic institutions fail to.

Also you have to be a fair way up the management tree before you have enough status or power to buy consultancy so purchasers in large organizations tend to be older. In life and in management, like tend to buy from like. Thus, to be the Perfect Consultant you have to be old enough to know things and yet young enough to deliver them. Old enough to know the answers, young enough to come up with new ones.

But being mature is not enough – there are some competencies required as well. As far as I know there is no research on the personality of the 'Perfect' consultant, but to succeed there are some behaviours without which it is unlikely that you will succeed. Not in any special rank order they are:

Persistence
You will need this to sell, to solve problems and to deliver with minimum resources.

Flexibility
No two clients are the same, even if you work for different units of the same organization. If your product or

service does not change to meet the needs of the client you die a slow double death of boredom and client seepage. Once you have been around for some time there is a great temptation to deliver off the shelf solutions. Don't.

Personal growth

This is flexibility again but not just changing things, rather changing yourself. If clients want standard stuff they can get people in their own organizations to deliver. Whatever your product or service, ensure that it is as leading edge as possible and that you know more than your client in your area of expertise – otherwise you become the other form of expert (ex is a 'has been', and 'spurt' is a drip under pressure).

More about growth later.

Opportunities

Consultants are like birds; it is the early ones that get the worms. You have to be able to see commercial opportunities earlier than other consultants, and there are lots of us, and, we are all pitching to the same clients. You have to work to real problems and real solutions, which is not always what clients initially think they need. Since most business (about 80 per cent after year 3) will come from existing clients, being opportunistic is essential for assisting clients in their fast-changing environments.

Controlled creativity

Every client rightly wants the right solution to his or her need without taking exceptional risks. Thus you have to have controlled creativity, for organizations are, in the main, risk-averse and the larger they are the more risk-averse they are. If you want to be exceptionally creative and daring then the realities of this world demand that your premiums on your product and/or service liability are paid and up-to-date.

Stamina

If you cannot drive 250 miles, deliver your product, service, advice or training for 7½ hours, drive back and start on the day's correspondence, then think twice about becoming a consultant. We don't work as hard as junior doctors, but you will get rushes. Even if you plan to work three days out of five, you will find that you work three weeks at a stretch and then have two weeks off. Clients, suppliers, the Revenue and Customs and Excise are very inconvenient sometimes!

LET'S BE NEGATIVE FOR A MOMENT

Many are attracted to becoming a consultant because they hope for:

Freedom
Recognition
Interesting Work
Independence

Freedom

Clients tend to be more rigorous and constraining than managers. After all they are spending their money, sometimes (hopefully) large amounts, and thus they are usually very specific about what they want and how they want it. Sometimes you get a project where the client tells you what the outcomes should be. The consultant is simply a scapegoat if the project goes wrong. You can make recommendations about how you would like to approach a project, but the client usually wants the quickest, simplest and, of course, cheapest solution. Academic research is more likely to offer you an environment where you can do things more thoroughly and elegantly than consultancy which is always challenged by those terrible demanding twins, perceived value and usefulness.

Frequently there is a time constraint – consultant solutions, answers and even training are delivered at a particular moment in time. Most projects tend to be about fixes rather than correctness, solutions for a particular moment rather than long-term panaceas. All this reduces the hoped for freedom.

Recognition

Like most service industries and functions you gain maximum attention when things go wrong rather than when they go right. When you do well the client rightfully takes the credit and when they go wrong you do your best to protect the client and absorb the blame as much as you can.

Interesting work

Aspirations here are also likely to be dashed. Most clients are conservative and will not want anything new, or at least anything which has not been tried and tested somewhere else, so we find ourselves very much the willing victims of fashion with organizations wanting to do what others have done or are doing. There are waves of consultancy such as customer-driven programmes, searches for excellence, quality, equality and re-engineering with the large blue-chip firms setting the lead and dictating the fashion. Consultants are rather like pilot fish helping the whales: if you cannot swim in the same direction you will have problems.

The work itself is interesting but not in an absolute sense, especially after you have run your twentieth change programme or introduced a communication strategy for your tenth firm.

In our experience most firms use consultants for implementing or doing things that they could very well do for themselves, but have neither the time, the resources or the inclination to do. One of us was employed in a publishing company to reduce absenteeism and had to do the necessary but very basic clerking job of stats absence figures!

Independence

Yes, as a consultant you get this but only in the long term. In the beginning you take on any work that you feel qualified for just to pay the mortgage and, frankly, to learn your craft by experience.

PERSONAL GROWTH

Somehow we expect our doctor not to smoke, our dentist to have nice teeth and our hair stylist beautiful hair. You live what you are, or at least your clients expect that. Consultants are expected to be on top of their subject or specialization in terms of qualifications, knowledge and experience.

It is easy when you are working to get stuck at a certain level and not keep up with your personal development. If you expect clients to pay a premium for your knowledge and experience then it has to be better than most.

This is easier to achieve than you might expect. Most managers only read one management book a year – notice we said read, not purchase! We reckon that if you read at least a book a month on your topic and one academic or professional article a week, you will find yourself ahead of the field. It is all in the books. Most consultants obtain a project, develop a product or training programme and then write the book and at all the stages write articles. Reading is the next best thing to direct experience. Jogging for the mind will create the same impression and confidence in your clients as when you go to a healthy doctor or to a dentist with a beautiful smile.

Where possible formalize your reading or studies so that you gain some qualification or membership of an appropriate body. Neither of us is particularly bright or top-drawer academically, but we have lots of letters to show how hard we work at keeping up with the intellectual Joneses.

It is so much easier these days with degrees, diplomas and qualifications gained by distance learning, and modular or credit formats. Not that degrees ever get you the work, but they certainly help you to get into 'beauty parades' for work. Qualifications give your work an added credibility (see the section on qualifications in Chapter 2).

Remember though, while it is important to be better qualified than the client, it will do you no good to flaunt it. At a recent pitch for some work with a leading city law firm the remark 'we can't use you, you would just intimidate our people' was made. On being asked why, they replied that it was because one of us had 'more degrees than a thermometer'.

So treat your degrees, qualifications and memberships like money in the bank – only you need to know how much you have and only get it out when you need it.

2

WHAT DOES IT TAKE TO BECOME A CONSULTANT?

'The race is not always to the swift, nor the battle to the strong, but that's the way to bet.' Damon Runyon.

Apart from technical and interpersonal skills, what else do you need?

MONEY

One thing you *can't* do without if you're thinking of setting up for the first time, is financial stability for at least the first six months, and preferably the first year. You may have to wait before fee income starts flowing in. If you've got a redundancy settlement or a legacy from Auntie Mabel you'll have some comfort. There's plenty of business out there, but it'll take time and you may have to wait a while for the regular pattern of work which brings in the sort of income you are expecting and hoping for.

So before you commit yourself to a consultant's lifestyle, analyse your financial position. What basic weekly/monthly living expenses do you have? Think about them under the following main headings:

> Mortgage/Rent
> Heating/Lighting/Water
> Cars(s)/Other transport costs
> Telephone
> Food
> Clothes
> Education
> Entertainment
> Insurances/pensions

Loans
Other

Then think about your set-up costs for the business:

Premises
Equipment
Furniture
Stationery
Telephone
Car
Advertising
Travel
Fees i.e. Accountant

How much do you need to earn to make sure these are covered? You may need to talk to your family about making some sacrifices while you establish yourself.

DISPOSITION

Chin up

John-Roger and Peter McWilliams' book *You Can't Afford the Luxury of a Negative Thought* applies to you. Acc-en-tuate the Positive. Optimism and a Positive Mental Attitude are the basics you'll need to take you through rejections and let-downs and fallow patches. The work is out there, there's lots of money being spent on consultancy – you've just got to find it or create the demand for it by believing in yourself.

Nose to the grindstone

'The need not to fail is the most powerful business aphrodisiac.' Michael Stewart

Michael Stewart, who set up the Centre for Crisis Psychology, now a thriving consultancy, maintains that the time to set up in business is when you have the most to lose. Then you really have to give it every ounce of commitment you can muster. Consultancy is not for the faint-hearted. You need dogged determination, self-control and lots of will-power.

Let's look at the statistics. If you're starting a marketing campaign and you have 100 leads, you might make 95 calls. About 45 of these calls will be effective. From these, you can expect to get 12 appointments to see prospective clients. Actual sales? Three. So in practical terms, the ratio of calls, visits and sales is 30:4:1. You should aim to make 40 prospecting phonecalls per week, six visits, and prepare three proposals. All this and delivering as well. When you land a meaty contract, you can't relax your marketing, or you'll emerge at the other end with no work. Most consultants we know are well used to working overnight, weekends, holidays and Christmas Day to put client proposals together or prepare training programmes or reports. In the early stages of your consultancy, be prepared to work 14 hours a day for six days a week, researching your market, looking for leads, writing letters, making telephone contact, following up initial communications, visiting, preparing proposals, following up and amending, putting presentations together, networking with your contacts and finally delivering your services.

The up-side is – you're doing this for yourself, and somehow that makes all the difference to your energy levels. Later, when you're successful and in demand, you'll have the luxury of saying 'Yes I know I'm the only consultant you want, and I'll be delighted to work with you, but I'm just off to Bermuda. I'll prepare your proposal as soon as I come back'.

Stay cool
1. Coolness in the face of pressure.
Often the client will take six months to make up his

mind that he wants a change programme, then he'll want you to deliver it immediately! This is when that old contact you chased up last week tells you he'd like you to come and present a proposal next week and another client decides he'd like you to run a team-building seminar a week on Monday. The life of the consultant is a bit like waiting for the Number 47 bus – nothing happens for a while, then three opportunities turn up at once. Juggling the demands is all part of the excitement of the job and My, does it feel great when you're in demand! That buzz gives you the extra energy you need to rise to the challenge. Smaller companies may need your services immediately; larger companies often take longer to make up their minds. So you need to get used to working in different timeframes for your clients.

2.Coolness when there's no work.

It's inevitable that you'll have gaps. Provided you're still doing your marketing – and you should be prepared to spend *half* your time on marketing in year one – there may be time to finish re-roofing the garage, learn French and catch up with your exercise regime. (Don't underestimate the importance of building a fitness programme into your weekly schedule – and see the short section on health below.) If your gaps get too frequent you need to re-group your resources, take a look at your marketing strategies and press on. Are you in the right niche in the market? What are other consultants around you bidding for successfully? Do you need to shift your emphasis? Your target businesses? Your target locations? Your marketing methods? Talk to friends, colleagues and associates. Scour the professional journals for current trends. Get an objective viewpoint and be prepared to change tack.

Stay real

Be ambitious for your consultancy, but keep a sense of realism. It might sound good to say your headhunting skills extend throughout Europe, but make sure that even if you don't speak the language(s), you have some influential friends who do, or your credibility will be questioned. Recently, some of our colleagues successfully landed a major change-management project with a Scandinavian company. Negotiations had been conducted throughout in English. As they finalized the deal, within two weeks of the start of the programme, they learned that one of the essentials of the project was to have a trainer who could speak Swedish. Fortunately, they had an active and extensive network and were able to find one and brief him within 72 hours.

On the subject of realism, we are Europeans now. Brush up on your linguistic skills – they will give you a positive competitive edge.

Flexibility
'Even if you're on the right track, you'll get run over if you just sit there.' Will Rogers

. . . *with what you deliver*
The perfect consultant loves change and innovation, isn't fazed by clients shifting the goalposts in the middle of the project and produces even better work when he hasn't had the chance to prepare it. All this comes with experience. But in the early stages there is no substitute for thorough preparation. As you gain confidence you can rely more on your natural instincts. Your reputation for being able to deal with whatever hits you on the day will grow and will enhance your client's trust in you and your business.

. . . *with when and how you deliver it*
Being a consultant means you can choose your hours, work when it suits you best, when you are at your most creative. As your consultancy becomes more successful you can become more choosy about how, when and where you will work, and for whom.

Warmth and friendliness
You'll need to get on with people, even when they can't make their mind up, don't get back to you, keep you late or keep you dangling. Even the highly technical consultant who doesn't work with people will need them to get the job in the first place. So unless you're the only person in the UK who can deliver the product – like the hydraulics expert who was brought in to the Manchester Palace Theatre from Yorkshire to mend the revolving stage on the first night of *Les Miserables* – you'll need interpersonal skills to get you past the first hurdle of making telephone calls and having successful first meetings.

Spotting the opportunity
Above all, you need the ability to keep your antennae on the alert at all times. Every time you talk to someone there is an opportunity of some sort. One of my neighbours put me in touch with a lucrative piece of work at the street barbecue. Like a policeman, you're never off duty. We talk about the importance of networking later.

Management skills
You'll need to organize yourself efficiently, keep several plates spinning in the air at once and be practised in project management. You'll need to keep on top of your business and have a clear idea of where it's heading, especially in those busy periods when you are out on the road. You will need to consider carefully what administrative support you will need to handle your VAT, invoicing and other financial commitments.

Positive mental attitude
Yes, you can do all of the above and more. There are a great many highly successful consultants who prove that going out on your own actually pays off. There is no magic art. You are uniquely experienced. No-one can do precisely what you do. Go out there and sell it!

HEALTH

Keep to a regular fitness regime. If you are a one-man/woman band, you may not be able to find a substitute at the last minute if you fall ill. Some accidents can't be foreseen (like the recruitment consultant who strained his back and had to interview all his clients while lying flat on the floor). Since you have to keep going, irrespective, make fitness a mandatory part of your lifestyle.

THE GLAMOROUS LIFE

'Those who lose dreaming are lost' Australian Aboriginal Proverb

When you first start thinking about consultancy as a career, you focus on the up-side. What are all these benefits?

- You're your own boss, in charge of your own destiny
- You do what you're interested in
- You choose who you work for
- Your home is your office
- You choose your working hours
- You decide what you're worth and how much to charge
- You can project your image, not that of the Company
- Your income ceiling is limitless
- The money you earn will go further

All this is 100 per cent true, but let's look at the other side of the coin.

THE PRESLEY PRINCIPLES

Are you lonesome tonight?

You're on your own now, entirely responsible for your success or failure. It can feel lonely without those old work colleagues you used to chat things through with. Identify a source of mutual support right now. It will help you maintain your perspective and balance and will give you an audience, for example, to rehearse your marketing strategy.

Jailhouse Rock

Just when you need peace and quiet to finish that proposal to catch the first post in the morning, the neighbour's teenagers decide to have a party. Or Susie next door decides to practise her trombone while you're telephoning the Chairman of Bloggs Brothers. Tell your neighbours what you're doing. Ask for their co-operation – maybe a quiet hour from 11-12 for you to make crucial phone-calls.

Heartbreak Hotel

How many hotel rooms do you know between Brighton and Caithness? You'll get to know lots more, and not in the most exciting places. Either use the experience to network and make some more contacts in the area, or indulge yourself with your favourite meal and a good book and have an early night. Make hotel stops the regular opportunity to find a swimming pool or gym and catch up on your exercise. Learn a language, keyboard skills or brush up on your marketing techniques.

In the Ghetto

Lack of resources takes a lot of adjusting to. If you've been used to having administrative backup, a secretary, photocopier, fax, PC and electronic mailing system, you're in for a shock. The basics you'll need are a PC to produce your correspondence and access to a photocopier nearby.

Wooden Heart

'If you want the rainbow, you gotta put up with the rain' Dolly Parton

When you're in business on your own, it's you the client chooses. It's also you he rejects. Disappointments are difficult to face, particularly when you know you're good *and* economic. Learn to face rejection in a more detached way. Imagine you're looking through a glass screen at yourself. What does the situation look like from the outside? Practise this exercise; it'll help you detach yourself from the feelings of rejection and prevent you feeling 'all shook up'. Tell yourself it isn't *you* they don't want; it's your product. Alternatively, give your company a name which is distinctly different from your own – GBH Enterprises or Potential Associates – to remind yourself of the boundary between yourself and the business.

PEAKS AND TROUGHS

This is what consultancy is all about. We decided to set aside some time in August to write this book, on the basis that nothing ever happens in consultancy in August. Big mistake. After a quiet start to July, several proposals came in, a number of sought-after meetings materialized and the work flowed in.

When you start out in consultancy, there is never a time when you have 'just the right amount' of work. Either you're 'resting' or you're trying to handle six jobs at once. Clients are never quite considerate enough to want you just after you've finished one job and before you are committed to the next. This is part of the frustration and part of the fun.

However, early on in consultancy you have to make some hard-nosed decisions about your own private time. Is it infinitely flexible to accommodate clients? Or are there limits? What, specifically are those limits? How does this affect the family?

We know many consultants who are so nervous about

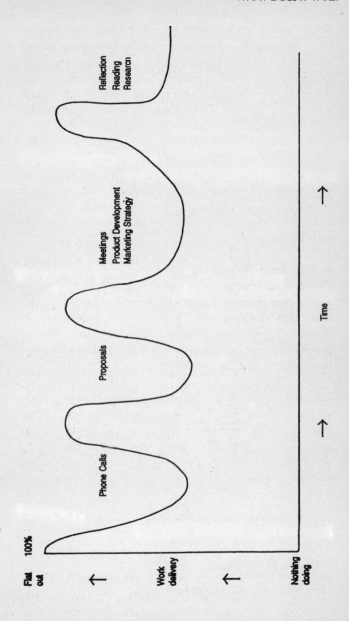

Figure 1 Using Your Peaks and Troughs

missing a potential opportunity that they do not allow themselves any free time, never turn anything down and ring home every day from holiday to see whether clients have been in touch. Or alternatively, spend every waking moment wondering what jobs they might have been picking up if they hadn't got on that plane.

You'll need to be very flexible early on. But put an end-date on it. After a year have a holiday, whatever the state of the business. You'll need it to keep your stamina levels high for the next phase.

Use your troughs to develop your contacts, to net-work, to develop your product and your marketing strategy. You should never be idle during a trough, un-less it is planned idleness – a proper holiday break. And *never* admit to a client that you haven't got much work.

Eye to the future

Planning in outline the way your business will extend and expand is an essential part of keeping on track. The perfect consultant thinks ahead. This way you can spot and seize any opportunity which presents itself as a means of developing your business. Decide where you are going. Are you going to consolidate one product/ one person? Or are you going to expand into several areas of consultancy and team up with other consultants to achieve it? What training courses are you going to take to equip you to extend your product range? What wider reading? Additional Skills work? Your own Personal Development never stops.

All hands to the pump

There'll be times when the whole family will be photo-copying training manuals, stuffing envelopes and answering phones. Give each member of the family their job. Train the children to be quiet when you're on the phone to clients and to be polite and business-like when they answer the phone. Write them a script and leave it by the telephone for when they take your calls, something like:

'Good Afternoon, John Green Associates. How can I help you? . . .
. . . I'm sorry, Mr Green isn't available at the moment; I'm expecting him back later this afternoon. Could I take a message, or ask him to ring you? . . .
. . . Could I have your name and the name of your organization? . . .
. . . May I check the spelling? . . .
. . . And your number is? . . .
. . . Could I repeat the message to you, to check that I have it right? . . .
I'll pass your message on to him and ask him to ring you back as soon as he comes in. Thank you for calling. Goodbye.'

Ensure that there is always a pen and a message pad next to the phone. Fix a notice-board with pins next to the phone and get everyone into the habit of sticking *all* messages on it immediately. It is safest to ban children under 14 from answering the phone unless you can be absolutely sure that they will always handle it professionally. Bear in mind that maturity of years is not always a guarantee of a professional approach either. A colleague tells the story of a chatty and friendly elderly relative who was in the habit of asking clients for all manner of personal details which were totally inappropriate for a business call.

SELECTING YOUR CONSULTANCY NAME
According to Shakespeare a rose smells sweet whatever it is called, but naming your consultancy has more significant implications. It is all about image again. What message do you want to convey when clients and

potential clients hear the name of your consultancy. Do you want to promote yourself or your product–cum–service or both of these things?

Naming anything is a very important step. Just look at one of the first things Adam did in the Garden of Eden, or the hours of family debate taken over the naming of a child. Your consultancy, like your child, needs a special and unique name. Here are just a few options:

Naming the consultancy after yourself
You can be The Alice Smith Consultancy
              Alice Smith and Associates
              Alice Smith and Company
              The Alice Smith Group

This was very popular in the 1970s and early 1980s and is the most common form of consultancy name.

Whilst it might sound egotistical, the client knows what he or she is getting. As you grow or get the larger contracts it is easier to present other self-employed consultants under your banner.

Terms such as 'and Company' or 'Group' make you sound bigger and more substantial than you actually are, and that might be important to you in the beginning. Some clients do have reservations about using smaller consultancies because, falsely, they believe that smaller outfits are more transitory.

After yourself and your partner(s)
You can be Smith and Jones
              Smith, Jones and Associates

This makes you sound more substantial. A colleague who first tried to present herself to a City law firm discovered that she did much better when she presented herself as part of a partnership, in spite of the fact it was a sleeping partner.

An interesting observation made by a colleague was that the inclusion of a Scottish name gave your firm a more substantial and upstanding image. On reflection this was certainly true of some of the large accountancy practices before the merger mania of the 1990s.

Initials
You can be ASC
       ASA
       The AS Group

The difficulty here is that initials do not mean anything so it is difficult to convey an image or a message unless your acronym is always used in conjunction with its meaning e.g. SEA (for Siân Evans Associates).

There are some famous consultancies with just initials, such as KPMG and P.A., but they achieved their client base before they abbreviated their name to their initials. Sometimes initials of the consultancy stand for the service or product. TDA, for instance, stands for Training Development Approaches and not the initials of a person or partnership.

Regional or geographical name
Here you use your locality, for example:

       Sussex Publicity
       North East Consultants

Our view here is that such names are limiting. What happens, for instance, when North East starts working for clients in the home counties? This happened with a firm called Geordie Job Finders. Clients in the home counties might not be attracted to a north eastern firm either because they are not local or because they are not national. A regional name works more for products because there is a certain cachet about the Norfolk Duck Company or Kendal Shortcake or Sterling Silver – although by association Sterling Consultancy sounds upmarket. Geordie Job Finders now, not surprisingly, trades under the banner of GJF.

One consultancy name which impressed us was Saxon Ridge which, although it is a place, is not bound by regionality. But note the impression it gives of age and thus stability, and height and thus power.

Non-specific name
It is said that Richard Branson chose Virgin because it could be used with anything from records to airlines and all things in between. So you could have:

The Pilgrim Consultancy	giving birth to Pilgrim Services, Pilgrim Recruitment
The Raven Group	giving birth to Raven Gravel, Raven Holidays
Dolphin Associates	giving birth to Dolphin Publicity, Dolphin Print

Certainly this format could help create the right image, although Phoenix is somewhat overdone. There is the Tower Group in Gloucester, who are well known for outward bound and management training. A derivation of this is the use of a Greek or Latin name for your company, such as Metanoia or The Rex Group.

All these give great potential for consultancy logos.

Some names have traded on the name of a more famous organization, for example, Coutts, who are perhaps the largest outplacement consultancy in Europe. Access Insurance was a small insurance company in Croydon, but no one would think so from the name, and that alone made telephone selling much easier. Just ask yourself which sounds better:

Jon Jones Associates	or	Buckingham Associates
15 Buckingham Gardens		Buckingham House
Thornton Heath		Buckingham Gardens
Surrey		Thornton Heath
		Surrey

Once you start working for a client it is the quality of your work that sustains the relationship, but in the initial stages how large, permanent or reliable you sound is important. The name is the game.

Service or product name

Americans and Australians are very fond of this, so consultancies are set up calling themselves names such as The Centre for Stress Management or The National Quality Association. It is becoming more popular here. The British Centre for Hypnosis Research began life in a small business centre in Brighton where you can hire rooms by the hour. They did and look how big they are now.

Not only does it sound impressive, but it also helps the client identify the main thrust of your service. The Centre for Crisis Psychology in Yorkshire is a great example. The client immediately knows what they are about. If the founder had just called it Michael Stewart Associates what effect might that have had in the early days?

And one important note regarding names of companies or firms: there are various rules and regulations as to what names you may or may not use. *Business Names – Guidance Notes,* available from the Companies Registration office in Cardiff, explains the position clearly.

QUALIFICATIONS

These count. Consultants are expected to be formally qualified, which means degrees, post-graduate degrees and professional qualifications. Europeans, Americans and Asian firms expect you to be qualified. To get consultancy work abroad, you have to prove that you are well qualified.

If this is outside your intellectual grasp then join professional institutes, either on 'the grandfather ticket', based on service to the industry or the 'status' ticket. Some institutions are more picky than others, but you will be amazed how many consultants there are each day in the Morning Room of the Institute of Directors, each of us with business cards bearing our name and MIOD.

Letters before and after your name (the ones before are best) help, but they are no guarantee. Also, some firms in Britain still pride themselves on their amateur status. To combat this I have one set of business cards with all my brownie points on and one set in the other pocket with just my name. On the day I make a judgement about the prospective client and try to remember which pocket has which cards!

If you have lots of letters, and one of us collects degrees for fun and personal growth, then on your business card put all your numerous letters underneath your name in very small print, otherwise it makes your card look ridiculous.

Use your qualifications to join the appropriate professional society and their journals will, provided you read them, keep you up-to-date.

3

THE CONSULTANCY PROCESS

Consultants should be 'get, gobble and go' organizations. Act like a medical doctor where you work hard to work yourself out of a job. Clients are to be helped towards their goal or vision and once this is achieved they no longer need the consultant. It is a poor consultancy that breeds dependency in a client. Clients do not exist for the consultant's benefit, quite the reverse.

Each consultancy project is essentially the same in terms of process and it is helpful to know what the stages are so that you can move from one to the other and then exit gracefully. We would suggest the following:

> Making Entry
> Making the Contract
> Making Options
> Making Solutions
> Making Action
> Making Exit

Throughout the process the initiative for each stage change fluctuates from the consultant to the client and back again, depending on the project, the circumstances and the styles of the consultant and the client, but the whole process is much the same.

Making entry
It is usually the consultant who makes the first move, identifying potential clients who have a need or a problem that requires assistance. Usually there is some form of pain or inadequacy that needs to be resolved. Sometimes the client is fine, but needs to improve its competitive edge or image in the marketplace.

Just as there are failures in dress with certain styles being too *avant-garde* or too early in the market place, so too there are fashions in consultancy and it has to be timed correctly, whether it is the pursuit of excellence, customer care, quality or competency issues. Not only are there fashions but they move through the various sectors. If one large pharmaceutical firm takes an initiative requiring consultants others will usually follow. What usually happens is for external consultants to be the initial providers and once the theme is established internal consultants take over the provider or delivery role. Time management programmes are a good example of this and change management programmes look as if they will go the same way.

Some consultants came into this world 'perfect' and are sort after by firms because of who they are rather than what they provide. Into this category go Urwick Orr, Peter Druker and Tom Peters. But for most of us making entry is the hard process of continually presenting our wares in the hope that someone will buy.

By and large it is easier coming from outside the firm and being a consultant (even Jesus said 'No one can be a prophet in his own country'). It is easier to be a three-yard expert, ie someone who come from three yards outside the factory gate, than to be recognized as an authority in your own organization. We have found that the further you travel to the client the more impressive you are thought to be. One of us once worked with some Australian psychologists who were, as it turned out, far more knowledgeable on the subject. But because we had flown 12,000 miles our observations and comments on the topic received much greater credibility than they deserved.

Conversely, the consultant may have a very good and much needed product but fails to get in because the consultant is perceived to be too much of a salesperson.

Very few organizations, if any, want to be 'sold' consultancy because it is not an impulse buy.

Making the contract

It is critical that both parties are realistic about outcomes. Most clients will tell you that consultants are big on promises and small on delivery and most consultants agree that clients are big on expectations and small on budgets.

The first issue to be addressed here is competency. Are you competent to do the job? It is better to let go a contract at the front end than lose your reputation at the back end when you have failed to deliver. Secondly, do you want to work on the project? Some organizations want outcomes which are at variance with your values. For instance, during the mid–eighties one of us was invited to break a union. This was within our sphere of competency but the employer wanted to achieve it solely to reduce his manpower costs as much as possible. We refused and as far as we know the union is doing a great job protecting employees from a ruthless employer.

Once you have decided you can do the contract and that you want the contract, the next thing is to establish outcomes. It is amazing how many consultancy projects are begun without either party knowing what specific outcomes are required. Useful questions to ask are 'What are the success criteria for that project?' 'What do you want the future to look like?'

Clients often say that this phase of the consultancy is the most useful. They know they have a problem, or that things are not as they should be but are not quite clear as to why or how they would like them to be different in the future. It is said that 'establishing the parameters of the problem is 90 per cent of the solution.'

Whenever possible the outcomes should be SMART:

> Specific
> Measurable
> Attainable and Agreed
> Realistic
> Time bound

and the consultant would do well to agree these before the project is undertaken.

Not infrequently the consultant discovers that the client does not really wish to change or is not ready for the amount of effort, resources or budget that it will require. Frequently, and not surprisingly, clients want far more than is possible. They might expect you, for instance, to set up an appraisal scheme, which will also ensure that the company changes its management style from autocratic to participative, where managers will have to be able to appraise staff but also need to be competent counsellors as well. The consultant's role here is to clarify the real issues and to help the client focus on what is feasible given the time, resources and money available.

During this stage too the consultant is being tested for his/her capability, credibility, empathy and trustworthiness. Major programmes or corporate changes are not only expensive in benefit terms but represent risk to the decision-maker's career prospects and personal credibility if a major project goes wrong. The client has to trust the consultant to be able to deliver what is required. This is not only a question of capability but also whether the consultant can be left to work with employees or colleagues who are not necessarily welcoming.

Making options
Real consultancy starts here with discovery of what the problems are. It is here that the consultant earns his or

her fees for asking questions to assist in the problem diagnosis and prepare the client for confronting difficult issues. Oftentimes clients, like dogs with their bones or their fleas, don't in fact really want to lose them but somehow feel obliged to go through the motions.

Sometimes being an outsider makes collection of data more difficult as one is regarded with suspicion. People instinctively know that whatever the outcome it is going to mean some form of change, and most employees and executives are conservative (with a small 'c'). Usually in organizations people have invested a lot of time and psychological effort in getting their place of work (where they spend most of their life) the way they like it, so most change is not welcome. On the other hand, as an outsider, you can request and gain information which the organization would be hesitant to provide to an internal person.

In our experience most people in organizations know both what is wrong and what is required to put it right, but for reasons of 'face' or organizational status an external consultant is required to point out the obvious. Like the subject of the naked Emperor in the Hans Christian Anderson tale, corporations pretend and act as if that which is false is true, since they cannot tell an executive he or she is the equivalent of being naked.

Sometimes consultants are told what to implement. A management who knows what is required but would feel too exposed to recommend or implement the changes will often instruct consultants. If the project is successful all well and good, if not the consultants are blamed and the management unblemished. A large retailer who is noted for not having consultants – because they know best – employs advisors to work with them. They were quite frank about the outcomes they wanted us to achieve but wanted the consultancy to 'fly the flag for them'. We were told that if the project looked successful, their internal management would take it over. We knew what would happen if it didn't look successful.

One of us has been asked on a regular basis for a variety of clients, from the Health Service to Manufacturing, to run a 'team', but the unwritten legend was to give feedback to an awkward executive or team member who for a variety of reasons, from status to expertise or in some cases, just fear, could not be confronted with the unacceptable aspect of his/her behaviour. (See Unwritten Agendas, page 80).

The current state of the organization is brought about and maintained by a host of factors and it is important to identify as many of them as possible. We always find it useful to look at the reward systems in an organization to discover where the real pushes and pulls are.

Who gets promoted, and why and what for?
Who is thought to be the organizational man, why and what for?
Who has status in the organization, why and what for?

One of us was invited to work on a contract to change the culture of a construction firm and soften a very hard autocratic management style, but once we began looking at the organizational reward systems it was obvious that the executive wanted the image of being a progressive participative management team, yet the whole organization was geared to and rewarded for a totally opposite form of management – it was the aggressive, task-orientated, man-eating managers who always got promoted.

The end result of all the questioning and probing is to

generate a variety of different methods and approaches from which the client can choose. In our view it is very important for the consultant not to insist on a particular direction but to give the client the choice. Exceptions to this are when the consultant is hired for their expertise, say in Health and Safety or computing, where there is a correct solution and all the client wants is for his/her problem to be sorted. But it is rare for there only to be a single option. Most consultancy is about working towards solutions rather than giving exact answers to specific problems.

Options give the client choice and the exercise of that choice brings client ownership and this is critical in effecting change and achieving lasting success. Solutions without ownership are doomed to fail. This goes back to SMART objectives, particularly the A for achievable and R for realistic. Some consultants propose solutions which are either too sophisticated, anticipate difficulties which are unlikely to occur or are fashionable rather than necessary – they seldom win repeat business.

Making action plans

It is not only the road to hell which is paved with good intentions. Poor consultancy is the same. Consultants receive fees for getting things changed, or plans implemented. No client is likely to be satisfied with just a range of options, however creative or state of the art, because they are not solutions.

As a general rule the better your fact finding and problem identification, the better prepared is your client for the implementation stage.

Making Options and Making Actions are different in that in the former you usually work with individual probing and asking questions, whereas in Making

Action Plans one is usually working with groups of teams. There is good reason for this. Firstly, any agreed action is bound to have implications for other people and departments. Secondly, decisions made through group discussion enjoy a higher likelihood of success because individuals commit themselves to each other in their work group rather than to the consultant. Interestingly, groups are more likely to agree to extreme or radical concepts than are individuals.

Discussion not only builds enthusiasm and commitment but also generates additional ideas, solutions and implementation strategies.

The more people involved in the solution discussion the better. The person who usually knows best is the person who either does the job or is going to do the job. This approach has direct links to the Carl Rogers approach to therapy in that if you ask the patient what is wrong with them they usually know what the difficulty is and what is required, so continually ask your client(s) how they want to do things.

Through discussion, goals will emerge in line with the agreed project objective. It is critical to write these down and circulate them quickly to ensure that everyone knows what has been agreed. Then comes the important work of resourcing and putting names, budgets and times against what is required to be done. This again relates to the SMT aspects of SMART, namely Specific, Measurable and Time bound.

We usually find that this is the stage when the consultant should begin to withdraw from the project. Because of experience it would be easy for the consultant to lead the project team, but for ownership, effectiveness and for the executive decisions that have to be made, it is better that local management takes over with the consultant acting as juror or mentor (see section on the roles of the consultant, Chapter 5).

In this stage there are two important functions which the consultant can fulfil. The first is to ensure information and feedback is given to all those involved in the project and secondly, since no plan is ever perfect, to facilitate and communicate those inevitable minor changes.

Sometimes managers work so hard on the project that they forget to recognize and reward good performance by employees in the direction of change. Consultants can ensure that effort, commitment to work 'over and above' can be given the recognition it deserves. Praise from an outsider is frequently held in higher esteem than from immediate management.

Making exit
Good consultants leave their clients as early as possible to ensure that the client does not become dependent on the consultant. Rather like the doctor or dentist you make the patient well preferably with preventive activities and responsibilities undertaken by the patient himself and then let the patient get on with his life. It is the same with good consultancy.

It is appropriate to have some exit plan where the consultant phases himself/herself out of the organization, returning only on a 'clinic' basis. Internal consultants or managers can be trained to take over. On one project we had an end of project party.

It is important to have a definite end to a project. If there is not an end then the waters are muddied for the next event. Some firms like Parker Pen have an event each year looking at a specific topic. The project has a beginning and an end. When we worked with a hospital group on a leadership event we arranged a launch and a completion date on the basis that by then the more decisive leadership style which we had been working towards should by that date be part of the day-to-day management.

These then are the major phases we have found from our experience irrespective of the content of the consultancy. Sometimes it is useful to share with the client at the outset the shape of the project process. People are always more receptive if they are aware of what is about to happen. With fewer surprises change is usually more palatable, just as the dentist, when giving an injection, tells the patient he will feel a small scratch; somehow, notice of an events makes it more easily endured.

4

FINDING YOUR CLIENTS

They're all out there somewhere, and your market research shows that many of them want exactly what you have to offer. So how do you find them?

NETWORKING

'Activity is the life-blood of a successful selling process. Networking is probably the most effective way of creating activity.' James F. Lewin

The art of networking is now being taught in business schools. Networking is simply talking and listening to people, 'putting yourself about', opening up all the channels to every opportunity. You are never off duty. Every telephone conversation, meeting, seminar, dinner, sports session and social occasion is a chance for you to network. Keep practising and it will become automatic. People are interested in finding out what others do. How much more interesting, if you can help make their working life easier.

Make a list of all your contacts, no matter who they are. Focus on them for a couple of minutes while you write down their name, address, business and telephone number, and their partner's name and business. Your contact list can come in handy for any number of things: someone recently asked me if I knew anyone who could help them buy a piano. I didn't – until I looked at my contact list.

I recently did a spell of jury service and spent long periods sitting around with a captive group. Now there are a few more trainers, bank managers, small businessmen and women who know about my work. And one of them very helpfully supplied me with names and addresses of prospective employers for my job-hunting partner.

In summary, every time you meet a new contact think of how you can use the opportunity to:

- impress
- find out what they need
- find out who and what they know in your area of interest
- tell them what you do
- extol your benefits
- set them thinking how you can help them

And yes, you can do this ever so subtly without the double-glazing salesman approach.

PUBLICITY MATERIAL

'There is only one thing in the world worse than being talked about, and that is not being talked about.' Oscar Wilde

If you are going to produce a brochure to advertise your product, it should say

1. What you do
2. Why you are different from/better than the rest

The format can be anything from a simple double-folded page to a detailed glossy booklet. Our advice would be not to spend too much money on the gloss until you've established yourself and are sure that what's in there is long-term. Provided it's printed pro-fessionally or produced on a modern PC, you can make a good impression with an A4 folded leaflet, which covers the following areas:

- The type of work you do
- Examples of work you have already done

- The benefits to the client
- Your specialist knowledge and expertise
- A list of previous clients (if available)
- Client testimonials

When I was at the receiving end of consultants' blurbs, the brochures I liked:

- were brief
- were easy to read
- contained little jargon
- had a conversational tone
- left 'white space' on the page
- described the benefits to **me**
- gave à la carte menus, not plat du jour
- were honest and realistic
- were client-centred
- offered help for greater effectiveness, not an all-time solution to all ills
- showed interest in working from the inside, not 'bolting-on'
- did not assume I had a problem
- showed some understanding of my pressures
- described a partnership approach, with me in charge
- were creative, memorable and visually pleasing

Plain English

Keep your claims simple and easy to understand. Avoid jargon. It might sound impressive to say 'We offer a comprehensive, integrated hands-on overview of current thinking in the field of communication strategy', but what does it mean? Much better to say 'We will train your telesales staff in telephone skills'.

Above all, your publicity material must reflect *you*, so take note of what is good about other people's brochures but tailor it to *your* business and *your* style.

FOLLOWING THE MARKET

Keep a sharp eye open for changes in the marketplace. All your clients operate in the same market, and they will find themselves in the same situation at the same time. For example, if one Health Authority needs outplacement help, look at the rest of the NHS. An economic upturn means more recruitment; if Barclays is setting up Direct Banking facilities, then the other banks will follow suit. Then there are fads and fashions and natural changes of emphasis in the marketplace; for teambuilding, quality initiatives, autonomous group work, visions and missions. Keep in touch with current thinking by watching the professional press and talking to other consultants and clients.

SOURCES OF WORK

There are seven main marketing methods which will help you find work:

> Former Employers
> Professional Organizations
> Conferences and Seminars
> Mailshots
> Cold Calling
> Advertising
> Other consultants

Former employers

People who employed you once may do so again. Charles Handy's 'shamrock' organization calls for small core teams helped by wide access to consultants. Make sure your old bosses know what you're doing and how you can help them. Unless you have left them under a cloud, they'll feel comfortable with you and trust you. Your expertise and experience is known and you have 'culture fit'. They might also want to retain you so that you don't work for their competitors. A number of my ex-colleagues in Electricity Supply are now working for the industry in a consultancy role. Make sure that you and your former employer check out the Inland Revenue rulings on giving contracts to ex-employees. particularly following a redundancy settlement.

Professional organizations

Membership of the main professional bodies which support your work will bring you regular updates in your field, notice of meetings and conferences, articles about current trends and a handy Who's Who of contacts. Take an active role and run for office.

Conferences and seminars

These offer a relatively warm group of contacts with something in common.

- Attend the big events in the professional calendar where you are likely to meet business people in your line of work.

- Offer yourself up as a speaker at your local Rotary, IPD meeting, IoD Dinner.

- Hire a room and invite local businessmen to a free lunchtime or after-work presentation with wine and crisps. Or catch the worm early – the breakfast seminar is fast taking hold as a lure for businessmen before they get stuck into the day's work.

Follow up afterwards. Ring the people you didn't get a chance to talk to. I recently rang someone I met at a conference almost a year ago. She didn't remember me, but was happy to listen because of our mutual interest in the conference. When I told her what line of work I was in she said 'I'm so glad you phoned, I'm just doing some work on this for my MD and I could use some advice. . .'.

Mailshots

> 'I shot an arrow into the air
> It fell to earth I know not where'

H. W. Longfellow

Cold mailshotting gets your name in front of influential people and pays off sometimes as long as 18 months/2 years later. It does however need to be a good deal more focused than Longfellow's arrow! See the Appendices for examples of a good mailshot letter.

I recently mailshotted 200 MDs and Personnel Managers in the North West. Three months on, after following almost every one up with a phone call, I have had six meetings and have landed one piece of work. Not, you might think, a high rate of return. However, I am now getting telephone calls from managers who 'kept me on file' and are beginning to think they might use me.

Follow-up is crucial. State in the letter that you intend to telephone but *only if you are sure you can*. Estimate on the basis of 30 phonecalls per day. If you think you'll get bogged down in other work, and may not have time, then it's best not to promise.

Developing a mailing list

For a fee, you can get a mailing list of all the companies in your local area, or in your specialism throughout the UK. These can be obtained through your local Chamber of Commerce or from the KOMPASS Directory in your local library.

Alternatively, try:
  Yellow Pages
  Driving round the locality,
      noting businesses and their addresses

See the Appendices for a list of useful publications which will give you more information.

Cold calling

One of our neighbours, a successful salesman, advo-
cates the following strategy for making initial contact
with clients:

Monday Call at the offices of the client. Introduce
yourself to the Receptionist. Get full and accurate
details of Charles Smythe, the person you want to
make contact with. Ask her to call his secretary if
necessary to check details. Get a feel for the place.
Leave your brochure and card with the receptionist. Ask her to hand your literature on to Mr
Smythe and advise him that you will be writing.

Tuesday Write to Mr Smythe. Remind him that you
called and left your card and brochure. Include
brief details of what you can offer, and the benefits
to him and his company. Ask for the opportunity
to meet him to explain more fully. Say that you
will phone in the next few days.

Friday Phone Mr Smythe. Indicate that he is expecting your call. When put through

a) If he shows interest, close this stage of the sale
immediately by fixing an appointment.

b) If he is hesitant/can't remember seeing the letter,
tell him about your benefits and close by asking for
an appointment

c) If he is not interested, ask if he has a list of
approved consultants, and can you get on the list
for future reference? Ask if you can ring him again
in three months, to check whether his situation has
changed. Ask if, the next time he is in the market
for your type of services, you can visit.

By the end of Friday, the chances are that there is a file

with your details in it and you will be remembered when you next make contact. Using this method in an organized way, you can make up to 20 calls per day in one area. However, be careful that you set up only as many contacts as you can handle in the time. This method depends on rapid and methodical follow-up.

Advertising

Leaving a leaflet underneath the windscreen wiper of a car might be a very successful way of advertising take-away pizzas, but it is unlikely to work for the professional consultant.

The key questions are:

Who are you aiming to attract?

What will they read?

The answers to both these questions are likely to lead to magazines and trade journals. A good way of advertising yourself is to offer a very specific product as an introduction to your services, either free or cheap to get people to respond directly. Examples of this might be a half-day accelerated learning programme at a special offer price (to cover the costs of room hire), or a group brainstorm on improving profits through better communication.

Other consultants

Keep in close touch with other, non-competing consultants for mutual swaps or help. A one-person band is limited in scope. It's vital to network with other sole consultants and it's worth hitching yourself to a successful group bandwagon as an Associate.

If you are a good 'Presenter/Doer' but not particularly good at getting business, come to an arrangement with a good 'business getter', who can open doors for you when he/she is looking for work. You can reach an agreement to benefit both of you – he/she gets 10 per cent or 20 per cent of your daily rate as an introduction fee and you play to your particular strength of going in when the client is already interested to bring in your expertise and to discuss the nitty gritty of the project. Similarly, if you are a good 'door opener', and are less interested in the actual delivery, ensure that you benefit from having a network of consultants whom you can charge for introductions.

A word about consultant directories

There are a number of directories which list consultancies and the services they offer. They are up-dated annually and include:

The Executive Grapevine

Consulting 1994 – The Official Yearbook of IMC (Institute of Management Consultants)

Human Resource Management Yearbook – Consultant Edition

However, they are expensive and unless you can get free access to them in your local library, don't bother.

Some other marketing methods which are worth noting include:

  Sending out newsletters to existing and prospective clients

  Writing articles

  Writing books

  Appearing on radio or TV

Always make sure that when clients contact you, you ask how they got your name. And once they begin to show an interest, keep them committed.

Using the 'hook'

The scene is a busy butcher's shop. A long queue has formed which reaches to the door. People are getting impatient. One or two look at their watches and start to shuffle their feet. Suddenly the butcher looks up smilingly and catches the eye of the lady at the end of the queue near the door, and says 'Good morning Mrs Ratcliffe, lovely day. I'll be with you in just a few minutes.'

What do you think is the probability of potential customers leaving the shop without buying

a) before the butcher speaks?
b) after he speaks?

I've just been advised that the landlord at the local adopts exactly the same approach. No wonder he does so well!

Getting clients to come to you

One of the most satisfying ways of getting work is when existing clients recommend your services to others. Maximum impact for minimum effort. A successful consultant colleague of ours does no direct marketing. Her professionalism is well-known and her services are in demand. The lesson is, always put the best of yourself into every job, no matter how small. You never know who you might be impressing.

THE COMMERCIAL NOSE

The perfect consultant is one who can catch the 'whiff' of an opportunity at a 1000 yards. There are many who can provide a technical service, there are many who are well qualified, but very few who can identify a commercial opportunity at an embryo stage.

We have tried all ways to get work and the least successful have been advertising, mailshots and inserts. It is much better to 'follow your nose'. We have two approaches which have rewarded us handsomely.

SECTORS

First, you operate in a sectorized marketplace which employs not only the same type of people, but also the same technology and delivers broadly similar products or services. Consequently as we've said before if one sector of the market requires your services, the whole market will. We have lots of examples of this. If you have a request from a Health Trust for Appraisal Training, then it is a sure bet that Health Trusts throughout the land will need Appraisal Training. If one pharmaceutical or computer company requires Outplacement Support, they all will. The reason for this is obvious. In an increasingly global market where there is considerable uniformity in the requirements of the markets to which they sell, the people they employ and technology they use, similar organizations will hit the same sort of problems at the same time. A blue chip company such as British Airways or Marks & Spencer will introduce a new programme for its employee's development, which will be announced with much fanfare. This programme then becomes fashionable and everyone jumps on the bandwagon, whether it is TQM or Customer Care, or Visioning for the Millennium. If you follow the business news and trade press on a regular basis you will soon see trends appear. Quickly do your reading, develop your product, run some freebie programmes with some of your tame clients, preferably those with credibility in the sector, and you are away on the crest of the next wave of consultancy fashion. But you must move quickly, for waves move very quickly and are dissipated very quickly on the beach. Nobody these days is running Management by Objectives, even Customer Care and TQM are on the decline. Surf with the next big one.

BEATING THE COMPETITION

For the second approach I have to tell you a story about an Asian client who was made redundant and came to us for counselling. He wanted to set himself up in business and we got to talking about Asian retailing. 'You know,' he said, 'we have a completely different approach to you English when it comes to retailing.' 'In what way?' I asked. 'Well,' came his reply, 'the English will walk down the high street and see there is not a fish shop and open one. It will go out of business within six months. On the other hand, an Asian will see four tobacconists and will decide to open a fifth because he knows that there is a market there. All he has to do is to be a better tobacconist than the other four and he will prosper.' We apply the same concept to consultancy. See what is common in the services that the competition are providing and deliver the same, only do it better. Marks & Spencer have been applying the same principle to their clothes retailing for years. They let changes in fashion prove themselves and become well-established before they launch a similar line. In this way they know that their product will sell to an already established market. It may be boring but it is profitable. Certainly in the early days of your consultancy let others provide the *avant-garde* and the leading edge stuff. Provide what everyone else does, only better, until you can afford to fly a few kites of your own.

COURTING THE CLIENT

The first phonecall

When you make the first contact with Company X, it will probably be with:

a) the decision-maker and holder of the purse-strings – the Chief Executive/Managing Director, or

b) the influencer in your area of interest – the Personnel Manager, Technical Manager, Finance Director, Training Manager

First, you have to get past the telephone operator, then the manager's secretary.

Telephone operator

Be courteous and friendly at all times. The operator will be able to help you get all the relevant information, like the manager's full name, exact title and regular office base. Armed with that information ask to be put through.

The secretary

The secretary is the key to your success. It is her job to screen out unwanted callers and to protect her boss. You might try to avoid the screen altogether by calling before 9am or after 5.30pm, when there is a greater chance that the boss will answer the call personally. Alternatively, during the working day you can maximize your chances of being put through by ringing at ten minutes to the hour. Meetings usually start on the hour.

If the secretary is there, use the full name of the manager you want to speak to. 'This is Andrew Short for Stella Graves. Would you put me through please?' Be confident that you *will* be put through. Smile while you're speaking. If she asks for information, be open. Enlist her help so that she is involved. If you cannot be put through, ask her to talk to her boss about you and find out when it would be convenient for you to call back. This way you keep the initiative and the control.

So you've got past the secretary. You're nearly there!
The prospective client will be making judgments about you from the first second you speak. Think how quickly we put together the life story of a stranger on the train, based on appearance and a few overheard words. Your appearance won't count this time, so the words and the way they are delivered will say it all.

Think positive

'Thou shalt decree a thing and it shall be established unto thee.' Job 22.28.

Before you speak, think positively of the outcome you want from the call. Use **affirmations** – personal and positive – and say them out loud. Practise in front of the bathroom mirror for stronger effect. (Your family will soon get used to it.)

'I am going to succeed in getting a meeting with this client.'
'I know that I am good – by the end of the discussion, he will know that too.'
'He will be interested in what I say.'
'I will make a difference to his company.'

Visualize success. Imagine yourself walking through the door into his office, shaking hands, greeting him face to face. Visualize in rich detail, using as many of the senses as you can. How will it look? Feel? Smell? Sound? Taste? Sometimes a vision comes to me, uninvited, and I know it will happen. This happened to me before I started to teach stress management and relaxation to others; I saw myself sitting in the group talking about the subject, the faces of the people, the features of the training room, even the clothes I was wearing. Other times, by deliberately visualizing something I want, I know that will happen too – or something even better!

Your objective is *not* to make a sale over the phone, but to get a meeting, by projecting confidence, assertiveness and a friendly approach. Above all, you are going to **enjoy** this telephone conversation!

Body language – on the telephone?
The listener can't see you but your body language will give out important signals which tell the client whether you are professional and confident or hesitant and terrified.

Smile
Your voice will be friendlier and your manner pleasanter if you smile as you say hello. The smile travels and the listener's comfort levels grow.

Stand up
One successful colleague says this always gives him a more authoritative tone of voice and helps him be more positive. He has noticed a clear correlation between stance and success at gaining meetings and closing sales. Radio actors usually stand.

Relax
Take a few deep breaths and a quiet moment to reflect on what you want to say. You will be more alert to possible openings.

So what do you say?

Introducing yourself
You are contacting a busy person. Check that this is a convenient time for you to call. Can he spare five or ten minutes right now?

Don't assume he has problems for you to solve, but remember he'll certainly be interested in improving his company's financial and competitive position. Come to the point quickly: who you are, the name and nature of your business and why you are contacting him.

Prepare
Have the start of your script written down. That way, you won't get tongue-tied, repetitive and boring. After a few tries, you won't need the script. You'll start to get a feel for what goes down well – changing the script to appeal to your prospective clients even more.

Pause
Use pauses effectively in the middle of sentences to give yourself a breather and to engage the client with what you are about to say.

A useful way to start

'Good morning Mr Read. My name is Angela Bright. I'm an independent Management Consultant specializing (pause) in training executives to manage (pause) Organizational Change effectively. Jane Freemantle suggested I speak to you as you are currently (pause) going through some changes in AFP Ltd. I'd be interested in exploring with you how you might benefit (pause) from using my skills and past experience . . .'

Positive use of referrals

The Jane Freemantles of this world are the opportunity-makers. A familiar name will increase the would-be client's comfort levels about

a) talking to you, and
b) making time to have a short meeting

So use your contacts –

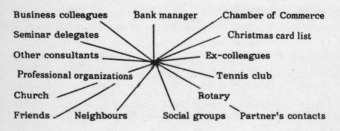

If you feel squeamish about using your friends, remember that you and they and their company may all benefit.

Name-dropping (1)

As a buyer of consultancy, one of the least effective phone-calls I ever received from a consultant was from one who told me (four times) in the first two minutes that he had recently struck up a warm friendship with my Chairman. He practically *insisted* that we meet. I felt pressurized and uncomfortable. He didn't get a meeting. Later, and not surprisingly, my Chairman said 'Geoffrey *who*?'

Name-dropping (2)
Be sparing in the use of the MD's name. 17 'Peter's in the first five minutes will sound overfamiliar, sycophantic and just plain desperate.

How much do you know?
Having some knowledge of the company you are contacting will impress the prospective client and assure him that he isn't just one of the 25 punters you've got on your hit-list today. Find out about size, turnover, numbers employed and product lines from yearbooks and directories in your local and college libraries and business schools. A small fee will give you access to a wealth of information. Read the newspapers and refer to recent cuttings about redundancies/share issues/expansions. Show that you are interested in helping *them* in particular, not just anybody.

Don't overdo it
There are few things more off-putting than a consultant who knows what the company needs better than the people who've worked there for ten years. Your role is to provide external expertise to complement *their* knowledge. Make a virtue of your objectivity. Peter Drucker, the extremely successful management consultant, maintains that he is hired largely because of his *ignorance*!

Striking the balance
You will be aiming to empathize or 'get into the world' of your client and help him see that what you can do will make a difference – to costs, to turnover, to morale, to the company culture. Show him that you understand his situation by reflecting back and summarizing his words:

'So what you're saying is ....'
'If I understand you correctly ....'
'You're indicating that ....'
'So, in summary, you ....'

Then move to the next stage and tell him how your services fill his needs. He needs to feel in control, so he will not take kindly to a line of selling which feels like a potential take-over bid. Rolls Royce don't need to market themselves aggressively. You can be positive without going into Used Car Salesman mode.

SPIN science
Neil Rackham, a psychologist, summarizes the selling strategy in the following way, whether on the telephone or face to face, using **SPIN** as the key to success.

S stands for **SITUATION**
> Encourage your potential client to talk about the current situation his company finds itself in. How long in business? How many staff? Struggling to be competitive? Reducing numbers? Cutting costs? Expanding rapidly? Recruiting? Going through organizational change? Expanding into Europe? Changing its product base? Diversifying? Being taken over?

P stands for **PRIORITIES**
> So what needs to be looked at NOW? Which issues are the most important? Where is the pain? What are the concerns? Changing staff attitudes? Increasing productivity? Culture change? Cashflow? Managers who are not used to commerce? Gaining commitment to change? Streamlining processes and procedures?

I stands for **IMPLICATIONS**
> Taking account of the Situation and the Priorities, what are the implications for your consultancy service? Which seem to be the areas where you might

help? How can you now respond to the client's stated problems and concerns.

N stands for **NEED**
The Perfect Consultant then identifies what the client's needs are in view of all the above, and offers it.
'It seems to me what you need is ....'
'Where we may be able to help you is ....'

You've taken the client logically through a series of thought processes to identify his important issues. He may be so bogged down with day-to-day problems that he has not clarified them until now. We recommend that you get used to this strategy; we have won hundreds of thousands of pounds of business through using it.

Try to get into the client's skin, and see things as he sees them. 'Walking in someone's moccasins' is how it's sometimes described. The more you can do this, the more you will understand how you can assist the client and clinch the deal.

An intervention strategy
Decide what part you will play in the client's world. Are you solving his problem or helping him with his thinking? Make it clear that you are not taking over the management of his organization. This will delight some and disappoint many, particularly where there are unpopular decisions to be implemented.

Keep your boundaries clear; you may identify issues on which to base future work. Keep the projects separate to encourage an on-going relationship.

If you can't help, think of someone else who can. Trying to be all things to all people doesn't work. Be prepared to admit if you can't help, and provide the name of a non-competing consultant, just as a doctor refers a patient to a specialist.

A word in edgeways

Most people prefer to speak rather than listen. Leave plenty of opportunities for your client to speak. The balance between talking and listening should be about 40/60, you/him. One sales consultant who phoned me from a large and prestigious consultancy group spent half an hour telling me about his organization, and didn't once stop to ask about mine. That spoke volumes about his approach to any work he might do for me.

A final word

Don't rubbish your competitors. You're not in party politics. Recognize your competitors and then stress the benefits of using your consultancy.

THE FIRST MEETING

Remind yourself that the client will be asking himself:

- Does this person understand my needs?
- Do I need this type of support?
- Do I trust and like this consultant?
- Is this consultant technically competent?

Prepare

The importance of preparation can't be over-empha-sized. Immerse yourself in the environment of the company you are visiting, at the very least sending for the Annual Report and Accounts, reading papers and trade journals and anticipating discussion topics.

Get there early

Even if it means getting up at the crack of dawn or stay-ing overnight. Motorway Coneland is something we're all used to and clients will make allowances, but you haven't got any brownie points in the bank yet, so deductions put you in the red. (The mobile telephone is worth investing in to keep your lines of communication open in hold-up situations.)

Get to Reception early and take in the atmosphere for ten to 15 minutes. Read the company newsletter. What clues do you pick up from the staff who walk through? How are visitors treated? What adjectives describe the company? Solid, professional, disorganized, dynamic, thrusting, creative, arty, relaxed, co-operative, tense, focused?

Best behaviour at all times
Don't underestimate the influence of the gateman/receptionist. During my years in personnel work, I often made a point of asking a receptionist about visitors. What a revelation! And never be tempted to flirt with the receptionist – keep the charm within acceptable limits.

In the room
Greet your client positively and with a smile. She is on her territory and she's in charge. Make a mental note of the layout. If it isn't obvious where you're expected to sit, let your client show you. I recall vividly and with embarrassment a meeting with a very charming client where I spent the first half-hour in his chair. Only when his secretary brought in the tea and looked surprised did I realize that I'd bagged the high-backed executive chair and left him with the lower status visitors' seat!

Kicking off
Let the client dictate the pace. Ask her how long you have. Place your watch on the table to show that you will stick to the time. You're one of her many commitments today. Encourage her to talk first, about her company, her position and her issues. Otherwise, you

run the risk of being asked what you do, how much it will cost, and being given a polite 'Not today, thank you'. Cover the main points you want to make within the remaining time available. Remember the importance of the client's comfort levels.

What you need to know

1. The background of the company. What changes is it experiencing? What challenges? You have already established some relevant facts before and during your first telephone conversation. Use these now.

2. In which areas can you make a difference? If a large-scale organizational change programme is called for, what will your individual contribution be? Who do you know who can handle other parts of the project? Can you project manage the work of others, advisors, trainers, facilitators? Or do you know of someone who can? Are you willing to work alongside other consultants already in place?

3. How will you and the client measure success? When numbers are reduced? When absenteeism has halved? Or are the measures less quantifiable? What qualitative measures can you set yourself? Have suggestions ready for your client; she will be interested in **outcomes**.

4. Who will you be working for? And who will deputize in their absence? You need to know who the key players are in this organization, and take your lead and your instructions from them.

During this process, imagine yourself as the client. What do the benefits look like from where she is sitting?

Save some for later
We remember very vividly being asked to attend an exploratory meeting with a potential client, who then

Howells Electrical –
Meeting with MD – 24 April

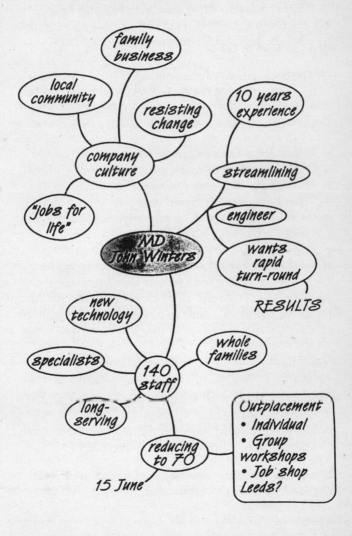

Figure 2 Using a mind map

very cleverly proceeded to pump us for all our knowledge and advice on the subject in hand. We were so accommodating that he had no need to invite us back. We learnt from that experience to give just enough, but not too much, information in the early stages – enough to whet the appetite for more on a fee-paid basis.

Listening

Have your antennae on alert at all times for openings. Ask open questions, which lead to discussion, rather than yes/no answers. Listen to the client. Ask yourself:

- What opportunities are here for me?
- Are they different from what I expected?
- Have I got the central message?
- Was I distracted by anything?
- Am I using methods of remembering which work well for me?

If you haven't got a good memory, read Tony Buzan. Or Harry Lorayne's book *How to Develop a Super Power Memory*. That powerful right brain can help you. And jot down the main points of the discussion as you go along; even superpower memories need the odd notes.

You might wish to record the main points of your discussion in a mind-map (see Figure 2). Most conversations don't cover each point logically and chronologically from A to Z, no matter how good the agenda is. You can add on bits to the relevant branch of your map, and usually you can capture all the information on one easy-to-refer-to page.

Use basic listening techniques to show that you understand the client.

- Empathizing:
  'It must feel very threatening for a well-established

traditional company like Percivals to face such competition from Japan. . . .'
- Reflecting back what she has told you:
  'So your company really needs to hot up its publicity drive. . . .'
  'You're looking for a Quality Initiative. . . .'
- Summarizing what has been said so far. (Use this technique part-way through the discussion to check your understanding, and then at the end to make sure you have picked up the most crucial issues):
  'In essence, you are saying that the company is faced with greater competition than ever before, with fewer staff and other resources. . . . .and that you need help in improving productivity.'

Don't overstay your welcome

Your prospective client has set aside a limited time for your discussion. Respect that. But don't leave until you both know what comes next. Say what you would like to do. 'I'd very much like to put a proposal together based on the needs we've identified together today. I'll drop you a line in the next couple of days with my thoughts.' Establish what level of detail your client likes in a proposal, and ask if you are in competition with any other consultancies. If you are very busy that month, you may have to juggle the 'dead certs' with the ten per cent chances, and spend your time according.

Record the events of the day

'I always say, keep a diary and one day it'll keep you.'
Mae West

Whether you use a mind–map or another favourite memory aid, no matter how busy you are, make a note of what was said. It's a bit like your contact list, things will pop out of it when you need them and the client will be impressed that you remember the conversation you had. Make a note of things you could have handled better. This discipline will teach you a great deal about yourself and you'll constantly be honing your influencing skills.

Make a note of company dress. Was everyone wearing formal black and navy? Or were there plenty of creative and colourful variations? Cream suits, cravats, pale grey shoes? Design a client contact form for yourself, and fill it in after every meeting.

The Appendices show an example of a client contact form

Thank you letter/proposal
As soon as you get back to the office, write and thank her for the meeting. Even if the proposal isn't ready yet. Then prepare the proposal while it's still fresh in your mind.

THE PROPOSAL

Purpose
The proposal is the sales document which restates in writing what you have discussed with the client. It forms the basis of the contract. So make sure it lines up with what you both agreed and that it doesn't contain substantially new information. Your client must understand precisely what you are offering and it must seem familiar.

The proposal outlines clearly what services you will provide, when you will provide them and how much you will charge.

Size
Proposals vary in size and style. The most important thing to remember is that your client is busy – and human. A thick tome full of wisdom might be appropriate for the reference library. It's not appropriate for

the busy executive who probably has half a dozen other proposals to look at. Think of the client's comfort level. Keep it brief, succinct, informative, imaginative. A former boss of mine refused to read anything which covered more than two sides of paper.

Layout

COMPANY BACKGROUND

Start your proposal by setting the scene. Summarize the company's current situation. It will be instantly recognizable to the client and will remind him how well you understand the company's issues.

OBJECTIVES AND OUTCOMES

Introduce the services you offer, which are of direct relevance to the company's stated needs. State the **BENEFITS** of your work together with the expected outcomes.

DETAILED SERVICES

Describe your services, whether they be training programmes, consultancy discussions, research or other offerings. Discuss the methodology you will use and why you have chosen it. Emphasize your Unique Selling Points (USPs). Pre-empt what your competitors will be saying and show why your benefits outweigh those of others. Refer to any manuals, reports and written analyses which will be produced/distributed during or at the end of your project.

TIMESCALES/PROJECT MANAGEMENT

Computers with sophisticated software packages are commonly used nowadays to manage large projects requiring co-ordination of hundreds and thousands of different work elements which all have to be brought together to make the project a success. Imagine trying to hold the plans for the reconstruction of Hong Kong Airport in your head or on the

CLOSURE OF LONGFORD FACTORY: STAFF RELE.

	EVENT	D A Y S	MARCH
			6 13 20 27
1	Management Awareness Seminars	10	
2	Staff Awareness Seminars	18	
3	On-site Careers Centre	62	
4	Job Search Workshops	18	
5	Self-Employment Workshops	9	
6	One-to-one Counselling (as required)	10	
7	Steering Group Meetings	4	O
8	Management Reports	4	
9	Project Co-ordinator	80	

Figure 3 Gantt Chart/Key events schedule

ROGRAMME GANTT OR KEY EVENTS SCHEDULE

APRIL	MAY	JUNE
3 10 17 24	1 8 15 22 29	5 12 19 26

back of a cigarette packet! Or the scheduling of the next Space Probe at NASA! For the hundreds of thousands of separate items and resources – including people – necessary for those contracts, it would be impossible to function without some kind of critical events chart.

To help you plan your project efficiently, plot the key events into a key event schedule – or GANTT chart (named after the man who introduced them). You don't need a computer and complicated and expensive software. A simple manually-drawn schedule is often all you need. It will keep you on track and will impress your client.

FEES
Indicate the fees you will be charging for each element in the project, together with information on how you will require payment, for example, payable at end of project/monthly in arrears/based on work in progress/one third payable up-front. This is particularly important if you need to do a lot of preparation and buy equipment or have teaching manuals printed and bound. Clarify what is excluded, e.g. additional printed manuals/VAT/expenses.

CLIENT LIST
Potential clients are often impressed by seeing who you have worked for before, and may ask you to address this directly in your proposal. Even if they don't, it is very useful at the end of your proposal to include a list of current and past clients for whom you have worked. Always make sure that these clients are willing to be listed and approached before mentioning them in your literature. It is useful to have some quotations from satisfied customers.

EXAMPLES OF SUCCESSFUL PROJECTS

Outline recent relevant work. (If you have no directly relevant experience, look for a thread of similarity which gives confidence that you can do it.) Examples:

'We have recently completed a comprehensive review of the Staff Appraisal System in a major petroleum company. We interviewed directors and senior managers and their staff in head office and nominated depots prior to redesigning the documentation. We then trained key managers and supervisors in the use of the new system and coached internal personnel staff to cascade the training throughout the UK.'

'Faced with major staffing reductions involving managers in a large and highly sensitive communications exercise with their staff, a recently privatized utility asked us to facilitate the change process. We designed and implemented an interactive workshop which dealt with the practical and emotional issues confronting managers and staff. Managers agreed that it was an invaluable tool in preparing them to communicate difficult messages.'

See the Appendices for a suggested format for a proposal.

The tender process

You may be asked to produce a proposal in response to a tender. The formality of the procedure means that you can have no contact with the decision-makers before the final decision is made, otherwise your tender is rendered nul and void. In all other cases (i.e. the majority), ring your contact and briefly go through what you have proposed, to check that it is what they are looking for. This gives you a valuable opportunity to tweak the proposal to make it even more attractive. If you're addressing a Tender Specification, work through the Spec. in the order the client has prepared it. This will help them to evaluate it. If this is not the case – sometimes Specs are so muddled it's almost impossible! – then answer it simply in the most straightforward and comprehensible way.

Spell it out

Remember that your proposal will more often than not be passed on to other senior executives in the company, so make sure it is as clear to them as it is to you and your initial contact.

THE FORMAL PRESENTATION

Consultant beauty parades are a popular way of judging who to use, and if your proposal looks good you'll be asked back to flesh out your ideas. You might be addressing one person; it could be six.

Preparation is the key to success.

Before the day – ask what they want and make sure they get it

Ring the person who's invited you and ask the following questions:

1. How long have I got?
2. What proportion – Presentation/Questions/Discussion?
3. Is it formal or informal?
4. Will there be facilities for me to show slides?
5. Who will be there?
6. When will I be on?

1. How long have I got?

The client is likely to set aside an hour, or possibly an hour and a half to receive your presentation. Stick to the timescale. The chances are there'll be other consultants to see, and by packing up promptly you'll earn brownie points.

2. What proportion?

You may be given 20 minutes uninterrupted time to put forward your points, then 20 minutes for general discussion and questions from the floor. Rehearse your presentation with a partner, friend or in the mirror, with all your visual aids, so that you are confident you can do it in the time. If people ask you questions out of sequence, thank them for the question and indicate that you will deal with it at a later stage in the presentation. This way you politely keep control of the proceedings and avoid losing continuity.

3. Formal or informal?

Some months ago, my colleagues and myself gave a presentation to a prestigious blue-chip company. No expense was spared on preparation, script, coloured slides with exquisite diagrams and personalized bullet points, all copied and professionally bound five times, one for each panel member. We rehearsed . . . and rehearsed . . . and rehearsed again. On the day we were brilliant.

The consultancy group who got the job came all prepared for a formal presentation but asked when they got in the room how the panel wanted to play it. 'Let's just have a chat,' they said. And they did. Game, set and match.

This important thing is to learn from your mistakes. The jugglers among you will be familiar with the wisdom, 'If you ain't dropping, you ain't juggling.'

4. Facilities for visual aids

Check out what's required and what's available – projector, flip charts, whiteboard etc. As a rule of thumb, never try to get through more than seven overhead slides in 20 minutes. Practise beforehand. One unfortunate colleague realized as he started his presentation that all the slides were in the slide holders the wrong way round, so that the flaps closed back over the message when they were laid on the projector. Not designed to relax the presenter! When fortune conspires against you like this, it's worth making a joke of it and getting any embarrassment out of the way. On this occasion, the panel saw the funny side and he landed the project.

5. Who will be there?
If there are five 'judges' you'll need five copies of your presentation summary. The makeup of the panel will influence your script. Your emphasis will vary if you're addressing training managers or the MD, Financial Director and Contracts Manager. What will they be most interested in? What do you know about any of them already? Use that knowledge to your advantage.

6. When will I be on?
Ask how many other sets of consultants are being seen. Ask for the slot which is most likely to give you pole position. You're aiming to be seen next to last. This gives you the benefit of a settled panel, but not one which is anxious for you to finish so they can all go home. In a full day of presentations, ask for the 3pm slot. If there's a break of a few days between presentations, aim to be the last to be seen. The impact of the first ones will have faded after a week and you are aiming for the advantage of **recency**. We talk about primacy and recency later.

The content
List your key points. Better to put over a few vital messages well than rush quickly through several. You need to make an immediate impact – the first 30 seconds are crucial. Stick to the tried and tested method of:

Telling them what you are going to tell them
Telling them
Telling them what you've just told them

Mind-joggers
Cards
Use a small pack of numbered 5″ × 3″ cards with headings of the main points of discussion. They are unobtrusive and look professional. This way you'll engage with the audience, rather than reading a script.

Visual aids
List all the main points of your presentation simply and boldly on overhead transparencies or 35mm film. Address each of the headings in turn. The presentation will flow and you will not miss out anything important.

Flipchart
Prepare a flip chart in advance. As an alternative to transparencies, some presenters feel more at home with flipcharts, and they avoid problems with temperamental overhead projectors or bright sunlit rooms!

On the day

Dress appropriately – as much like the client as you can and if in doubt more formally. The clone syndrome influences selectors to prefer people who are like themselves. Refer back to the diary notes you made when you visited.

- Remember your **visualization** and **affirmation** techniques. Think positive and imagine your success.

- Anticipate the questions you are likely to be asked and prepare your answers. Look at questions you've been asked before and then ask yourself what's different about this organization. What are

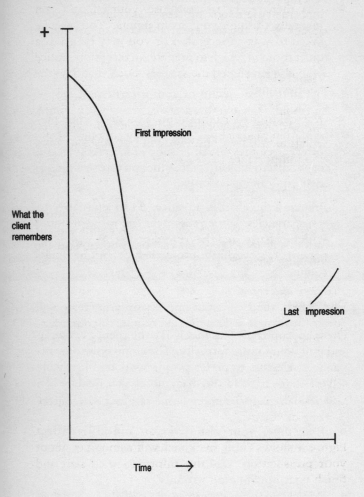

Figure 4 Primacy and recency

thcir particular concerns likely to be? Your specific experience? Money? Ability to sustain the project? Personal 'fit'? Flexibility?

- Get there early to compose yourself and run mentally through your main points. You may be asked to wait in reception or you may be given a quiet room in which to prepare. In reception, notice who else has signed the visitors' book that day (the competition!).

- Keep clutter to a minimum. You need your presentation material plus emergency supplies – hairbrush – clothes brush – shoe shine. Ask the receptionist to look after any other private belongings that you can't leave outside.

- Practice breathing slowly before your presentation; this will relax you and calm you and your state of mind will transmit itself to your audience in the opening seconds.

Primacy and recency

Fair or not, the long-term impression you create will largely be formed within the first minute of your entering the room – what is known as the **primacy** effect. This is influenced by three things:

Dress
Body language including smile rate and eye contact
Tone of voice

Figure 4 shows what the panel will remember about your presentation. Use this information to start and finish your presentation strongly.

Get your audience to participate in one or two questions in your introduction to gain their interest and involvement. Like the first page of a book, it has to grab their attention. Aim to inform and to entertain, varying the tone and pitch of your voice. When you summarize find new words and ideas rather than simple repetitions of what you have already said. Always emphasize the benefits to them. If at any point you are losing your audience, be bold enough to stop the proceedings and ask them 'Is this what you are looking for? . . . How many of you feel that this is a worthwhile approach? . . . Can I usefully emphasize another area?' This is not easy to do, but it introduces the element of spontaneity and surprise and shows that you are perceptive and flexible. End on a high note – a positive anecdote or a recent example of your success.

When your presentation is over, thank the panel for their attention and leave promptly. The presentation isn't over until you've left the site so maintain your professionalism at all times.

Keep a notebook in your glove compartment or briefcase. Before you drive away, jot down the main questions they asked you. Keep these in a file and read them before the next presentation.

After the day

Stay in touch
'When you get right down to the root of the meaning of the word "succeed", you find it simply means to follow through'. F. W. Nichol.

The following day, write to the company as follows:

- Thank them for the opportunity to present
- Confirm your on-going interest
- Fill in any gaps you didn't have chance to deal with or thought of later

This will have a number of effects.

- It will help to keep your name uppermost in their minds

- The additional information you supply might tip the balance if they are having difficulty deciding between presenters

- If shows enthusiasm and commitment to their project

See Appendices for an example of a letter showing how to keep in touch.

Follow up with a phone call a week after the presentation, indicating your keenness to carry out the work.

Whether you get the work or not, ask for frank feedback. What were they impressed by? What was the key to your/your competitor's success? How could you have improved your chances of gaining the work?

5

THE WORK OF THE
CONSULTANT

CONSULTING ROLES

Before you begin any project, it is wise to work out in advance what role you are expected to play in the provision of your product or service.

Flowing through and underpinning all the roles is an expectation that you will be an expert in your subject, but the way you will deliver that expertise will be different according to the requirements of the project.

The five most common roles are:

Expert
Teacher
Trainer
Problem identifier
Counsellor

We expand on these later, but other roles can include:

Go-between
Executive
Conciliator

The go-between can bring different factions or sides of an organization together. Unions and management would be an obvious example, but sometimes different functions, such as Marketing and Sales, or Research and Production need integrating, especially where they have been competing against each other for resources or have been led by antagonistic executives.

The conciliatory role is similar, but is involved where

there is a specific difference between two parties that needs to be resolved.

When an organization is going where it has not gone before, such as a significant restructure or a Total Quality Management programme, then the consultant plays the role of executive guiding the organization and the project in the direction required.

A few moments thought will tell you which is the most appropriate role for you within the project. Occasionally your role will change as the project matures. So, for instance, in a restructuring your role could move from executive to go-between to conciliator to trainer – all within the context of a single project.

A consultant is a person for all seasons and the perfect consultant is comfortable in playing many roles irrespective of his or her own style. The role should really reflect the need of the project, the client, and the required outcome, with the consultant being a chameleon continually adjusting to the needs of the situation.

Figure 5 shows the range of roles with the overall responsibility for outcome within the client/consultant relationship.

Figure 5

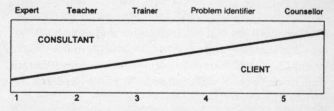

At position 1 the client is completely dependent upon the consultant to do the right thing and achieve the required objective. Here, for instance, the consultant could be an industrial relations expert representing the client at an Industrial Tribunal or a Health and Safety specialist advising on the guarding of a hydraulic press. A specific outcome is required and the client delegates total responsibility to the consultant for its achievement. The consultant is responsible for process and content, that is to say both the 'how' as well as the 'what' of the project. At this end of the spectrum the outcomes are far more clear and specific – but as you move from 1 towards 5 in the figure the number of potential outcomes increases and thus the client plays an ever-increasing part.

At point 2 the consultant is the teacher. The role here is to inform, give facts, impart information. Knowledge is transferred from the teacher to the client who then applies that knowledge to their own specific situation with or without consultant assistance. An example here would be a quality programme to achieve IS9000 or an inventory management programme such as MRP2. As can be seen the consultant has first to teach the client about the principles, facts and operational requirements before the client can implement the appropriate system(s) within the organization.

Midway on the vector, acting as a trainer the consultant shares with the client both the content and process. Learning is through debate, discussion and mutual sharing. The consultant may be expected to know more about different types of training delivery such as Role Play, Group Discussion, Brainstorming or similar exercises, but the real and significant input comes from the client participant. Process is guided by the consultant but content comes from the client. This form of consultancy has a noble tradition from Socrates to Christ whereby asking significant and provocative questions of their students provokes the discovery of the answers to the questions. Thus clients retain responsibility for their own learning and personal development and decision outcomes.

At point 4 the consultant is somewhat of a fixer or a linker. The client has a problem and the consultant knows who or what is needed to fix it. Here the consultant is rather like a catalyst in a chemical reaction. He or she plays no part in the reaction itself but because of his or her presence the result occurs much earlier. Oftentimes the consultant in this situation prevents the client having to re-invent the wheel.

A variety of tools can be used to assist the client in identifying organizational needs from questionnaires, audits, attitude surveys and structured interviews to observation, bringing to the surface in a formal way the organizational attitude agendas, which the client then needs to address. The role of the consultant is deciding which method will produce the highest quality information required by the organization given the situation, values and desired future.

Finally, at point 5 we have the counsellor whose responsibility is for process and not in any way for content. Here the consultant is totally non-directive using reflective open questions to challenge and confront the client so that the executive and not the consultant makes all decisions and movement towards resolution. In no way is the consultant responsible for the outcome but reflects back to the client his or her current position, and through probing, summary and reflection the implications arising from client decisions. In this way the client grows in both personal knowledge and empowerment.

This form of consultancy is the organizational equivalent of the psychiatrist's chair. In Chicago once, one of us was told by an increasingly frustrated client that he was going to cut off the arms of the writer first so that he would not hear for the 'nth' time 'on the one hand . . . and yet on the other hand . . . !'

Roles and the project
To be perfect the consultant needs to be able to move easily from one role to another and be comfortable in

working in any of the roles. In certain parts of the project the consultant may have to be the expert, say, in giving information about customer care programmes and their successes in other organizations, but then be a counsellor whilst the client decides how best the organization can move forward. Once this decision is made the consultant may become problem identifier followed, finally, by the role of trainer as the customer care programme is implemented.

Knowing which role is appropriate to which situation is frequently the key to project success. It is not easy for the consultant to forsake his or her natural style and it requires both skill and practice to perfect.

PROBLEM SOLVING

It is well to remember always that clients are not paying you to be clever, erudite or elegant. They just want a problem sorted. In our experience a lot of consultancy comes not from what a client can't do, but from what they don't have time to do. Advice here then is obvious – just solve your clients' problems in the most effective and cost-efficient way. If you want fame and perhaps fortune for your intellectual elegance then work in a research laboratory or university, but not in consultancy. KISS applies everywhere – Keep It Simple, Stupid. Not because clients are stupid – far from it – but they need simple, effective solutions. If you keep asking yourself 'How can I solve this client's problem in the simplest way?', you will find that your consultancy will not only get new clients through your reputation, but you will keep your existing clients who will be loyal to you because of your work.

CLIENTS WITH UNREALISTIC EXPECTATIONS

Sometimes clients think you can perform miracles. I was once asked to 'do' management in half a day with junior doctors. Apparently that was to cover leadership, motivation, style, team-building – rather like those tours sold in America where you can 'do' Europe in six days. I suppose we really ought to be flattered that anyone could think we had such skills.

Many clients confuse conceptual understanding with changes in behaviour. In the example quoted above I managed to convince the client we could 'do' leadership in a day. The doctors, being doctors, went through the theory very quickly and also picked up all the jargon words, but in the afternoon when we came to the case studies and the role plays, it was immediately obvious that 'brain aspects' and 'behaviour aspects' were very different. All that changed was the language and not the behaviour.

Clients are usually professionals in their own right and we are quite adept at first saying we could 'do it' in half a day, but how long did it take them to develop proficiency in one of their professional skills? Use that as an analogy bridge to explain how it would be better done with fewer subjects over a greater time period.

WHAT TO TAKE ON

On training programmes where there is a day fee, clients obviously want to maximize their value for money by getting as many people on to programmes as possible. If you can have 12 on a programme, then why not 15, if 15 why not 20, if 20 why not 30 and so on.

High numbers are possible if the content is just technical, and what is required of candidates is to follow a mechanistic process. I can remember lecturers at university presenting to 300 people at a time. Even with complicated facts as subject matter this is possible; the difficulty comes, however, when what is required is a change in attitude or belief systems or the way people do things.

Also managers and executives are not used to sitting

down all day soaking up information. Part of the job as a consultant is to do other people's reading for them. I reckon my attention span on technical material is only about 35 minutes at most. If I can keep a bright manager concentrating on a specific topic for 20 minutes I am pleased.

Where clients have wanted as many people 'processed' as possible, we have run seminars with up to 150 people, with a lead presenter and then one consultant sitting in with ten of the participants. It worked reasonably well, but not as well as if we could have had 15 separate seminars.

As a general rule in the consultancy we like to work on a 1:12 ratio for training groups, and 2:15 when there is a large element of attitude or behaviour change required.

It is better to walk away from a contract than get involved with something that you know will not work. The potential of repeat business and/or reputation is too great to waste on a programme which you know is doomed to failure. If you are honest with your client it is surprising how many of them will give you the business on your terms.

Unwritten agendas
It is not uncommon for us to provide 'team events', and within ten minutes of their commencement we discover that what the client really wants us to do is to sort out the obvious misfit who is not working as part of a well established team. Or the client wants you to promote an idea or concept about new methods of working or implementing new processes which are sensitive to the organization. For many reasons the management of that particular client have not, cannot or do not want to introduce the idea themselves. If you do well you have the client behind you and supporting you before they

take over the project, if you fail you are suddenly treated as a bunch of consultants who did not really understand the issues properly. Kite flying for clients goes with the territory of consultancy.

No top-drawer commitment
When there is no commitment from the top, consultancy inventions are doomed to failure – sauce for the goose, sauce for the gander. So often there is only verbal support for quality, customer care, participative leadership or empowerment, especially when such things are fashionable, and top management behaviour does not support, endorse or reflect the stated aspirations. If top management are not prepared to 'walk the talk' then walk away from the project.

In change projects we are now careful to secure a project champion from the top management team and we do all that we can to service the project, rather than be seen as the consultancy which leads the project. If there is no commitment from the top, we ensure that the success criteria for the project are as general as possible.

Walking on water
This is a real trap for a consultancy. Sometimes when a contract or project goes really well, you will get invited back to do another project, which is perhaps just outside your competency. The danger of course is that you accept it and then subsequently fail. It is much better to link in with another consultancy to work either under your banner or in partnership. It is flattering to be invited to do things but remember most of us have feet of clay.

Doing too much work for one client
We have a rule in the consultancy that we will not allow any one client to provide more than 33 per cent of our work in turnover terms. The reason for this is simple:

you become too dependent on that client and should you fall out of favour you are in danger of losing your consultancy. We have been close to our 33 per cent rule, but rather than reducing our work it has driven us harder in our marketing and sales activity. Like asking for credit, we have always found it easier to get work when we don't need it.

Beware standard solutions – yours

Habit is an insidious thing which roots itself in organizations as well as individuals. It is not always sensible to repeat successful projects with different clients. There are too many variables of culture and personalities for something to be repeated. Customize each of your products and services to meet exactly the needs of your clients.

Imposing your values

Most consultants have strong views and strong values for that is one of the attractions of going solo in the first place. However, sometimes there is a danger of imposing your value systems on the host organization, or that part of the organization with which you are working. We may believe passionately in participative management, a matrix management structure or a totally empowered workforce, but these are not appropriate in all situations. Just as the body rejects alien tissue so an organization will reject alien values. The job of the consultant is to deliver to the needs of the organization, rather than be an evangelist for its own world view. One is a missionary for one's clients, not for oneself.

Churning

This phrase comes from the City where shares are bought and sold when there is no need or gain in doing so for the client, but it makes the broker look as if he is working hard and often gains him extra commission. If work is low there is a danger for consultants to churn their clients to gain work which really isn't necessary. Going for a new project is fine if it works to clients' needs, but creating unnecessary work is one of the fastest ways of losing a client and your reputation. Clients take more interest in projects than most shareholders in their portfolios.

DOING THE WORK

Keeping to the contract

In our experience, the formal contract rarely appears. Our work is based on the written correspondence and discussions we have with our clients. The contract, or correspondence which replaces it, commits you to a particular piece of work to be undertaken for a particular price. It outlines your responsibility to your client and the responsibilities accepted by them. Sometimes, clients have a standard contract, which they adapt for all outside services. Some consultants, particularly the larger groups have their own standard contract which can be adapted to meet specific needs.

Types of contract/understanding

In general, there are two types of contract

1. Fixed Price Contracts specify a service which the consultant will perform for a known price. For example, a job shop on site at the company premises for three months for an overall cost of £x000. The client knows precisely how much expenditure he is committing from the outset. It is therefore important that you, the consultant, know precisely what your costs will be, as you will have no comeback if you have forgotten to add in the costs of a crucial part of your service.

2. Variable Price Contracts give you the benefit of charging for the actual work you do, to some extent working it out as you go along. For a research and development project, for example, the company may be prepared to be flexible, provided the total contract does not exceed a stated amount.

Keeping to the budget

In the early months of consultancy it is easy to underestimate the amount of time it actually takes to complete a project. Keep an accurate record. Have a file for each project and input your time and expenses regularly. If you over-shoot your budget, it's your problem, not the client's. Chalk it up to experience and learn from it.

Up-dating your client

Keep closely in touch and give regular verbal and/or written reports. This will ensure that the client feels in control, and that he is never wrong-footed when senior colleagues ask him for progress on the project.

Giving feedback and presenting reports

Your work may involve presentation of a report at the end of a piece of research. Refer back to your correspondence and check that you are fulfilling all your commitments. Are you being asked to produce recommendations to solve a problem? Establishing facts and setting out your conclusions so that the client can decide on a course of action? Have you agreed to produce a written or oral report? To whom? In what timescale? In what format?

Some forms of consultancy, eg. delivery of training programmes, do not call for an end of work report. Even in this situation, set aside some time for evaluating, with your client, the usefulness of your work. This will demonstrate your interest and commitment, and may lead to further work. Some consultancy organizations get 70–80 per cent of their work from repeat business.

6

COMMERCIAL ASPECTS

WHY ME?

In the beginning you have to do some hard work on 'Why me?', because the client will always ask 'Why you?' If you get to pitch for work the potential client will have two or three other consultants presenting their wares as well. The larger the contract and, sometimes, the larger the client, the more consultancies are invited to tender for the work. Our personal record was the MOD when 22 firms were invited to pitch for a significant contract.

Sometimes firms are not quite sure what they want so they invite quite a few consultancies, just to get their heads around the problem and understand the issues. Unfortunately, on more than one occasion clients have invited us in and insisted on a very comprehensive tender on how we would approach the work – so that they could do it themselves. With experience you learn to spot the less scrupulous client fairly early in the tender process.

When there are two or three consultancies, all with a track record of providing similar work, the client has a problem: 'Why should I select one as opposed to another?'

Clearly the client will make a selection based on his liking for the consultants concerned. But he also has to bear in mind the question 'Who presents the least risk?'. To help the prospective client reduce his risk, he will want to know:

● What similar work you have done.

- What similar clients you have worked for in terms of:

Sector	Projects	Values
Product	Geography	Standing
Size	Location	Experience
People	Attitude	

- What similar problems you have dealt with?

- Anything you have done which you can use to convince the client that you have direct relevant experience of what they want done, which will help reduce their perceived risk.

Before you present ask yourself the question, 'why should the client go with our firm?' Unless you are a very close personal friend of the decision-maker, you have to come up with as many reasons as possible.

Do not wait to be asked the question 'And why should we select you?' Build into your presentation as many 'when we' statements as you can:

When we did a very similar project for . . .
When we have worked in this location before we . . .
When we have worked with research staff in the past we . . .
When we worked with other Government Departments we usually . . .
When we worked in process engineering we . . .

You have to be careful because sometimes there is such rivalry between Government Departments, or organizations that to have worked for one will automatically bar you from working with your prospect. However, it is not that difficult to discover who the client's reference points are. Often your contact in the organization is not the decision-maker or budget-holder so it is usually possible to run your 'When we' by that person.

The question you should be asking yourself is 'How can I show the prospect that I understand their specific needs and that we can provide solutions that have been successful in the past?' Before one has an operation it is comforting to know that the surgeon has successfully performed the operation about to be performed on you many times and that the outcome was successful every time. Your presentation must have the same degree of experience behind it – or at least generate as much confidence as possible.

You might not like it, but think of your consultancy as a packet of biscuits with numerous other packets of biscuits on a supermarket shelf – why should the shopper buy me? What makes me special, interesting or different and yet just right for the customer? Once you have grasped this simple idea you have gained the concept from sales called 'USP' or Unique Selling Point (or Proposition). You have to know what it is that makes your consultancy the right one for this project, why you should be selected.

In preparing for any discussion about potential work you should always think through and agree what your USPs are. Here are a few we have used that have helped us win business:

- Worked for similar organizations
- Worked in the same sector
- Small and thus flexible
- Team members well trained in research
- What you see is what you get (WYSIWYG)
- Team has similar background to the people we will be working with

- Knowledge of the locality
- Geographical spread of consultants
- Quality of our support materials
- We are widely published in the area
- We are good value for money
- We have worked for the organization before
- Our reputation in this line of work

Each potential client will need its own USP profile for you to develop and the more experienced you become in the area, the more projects you are likely to win because you can deal effectively with the 'Why me?' question.

YOUR FEE STRUCTURE

How much you should charge is fraught with difficulties. Too much and you lose the contract, too little and you are thought too cheap to do the job. The most frequent mistake is charging too little. If you start low you stay low and your client recommends you because you are so low. Most people when they start forget to build into their fee the following:

How long its takes to win contracts
How much it costs to keep up-to-date
A sick pay provision
Your pension

Not to mention your office accommodation, secretarial assistance and, of course, something for yourself.

A simple formula is as follows:

$$\frac{\text{Your salary on the job market} \times 1.25 \times 3}{232}$$

232 is the number of working days in a year, 1.25 is to cover sick pay and pension and 3 because initially you

will work 1 day out of 3. I have always found that using this formula keeps you in the right ball park.

Delay talking about fees for as long as you can. The client knows you are not going to work for nothing and you know that the client would not be talking to you unless there was a project. The later the discussion about fees, the less of a problem there is for you because the client is more committed to the consultancy project.

Where you can, go for a project fee rather than a day rate. This is because on the latter the client will always pare you down wherever possible. Much better to have a straight fee. An added benefit to the project fee is that you may be able to get 33 per cent advance on commencement of the project.

Our advice is, do not negotiate on fees, it just makes you look amateurish. A client of ours was approached by a consultant to do some work and quoted £600 per day. The client flippantly remarked 'How about £100?', and the consultant, thinking he was serious, agreed! Needless to say, her credibility was shot and the project went elsewhere.

It is always useful to scan the bookcase of your clients because then you can see which consultants they have used before. I can vividly remember being pushed on fees by a health executive when behind his head I could see three or four A4 ring binders on which were emblazoned the names of first-division consultants whose charges were at least twice what I was asking. I smiled, looked the prospect in the eye, and said something like, 'We take a long time developing our fee structure because we want to be fair to you as well as to ourselves, and we know that our fees are not as high as our competitors. They would be if we had to maintain their profile and their city office overheads, but we would prefer to pass our savings on to you.' We won the contract.

If the client pushes you on fees then here are two tactics we have tried with some success. The first is to say something like, 'Well, we could cut out certain parts of the project to meet your budget – which parts do you think could be cut?' On reviewing the project the client usually finds that he or she wants the whole ball of wax and somehow finds the money. The next task is to suggest that we use some of the client's personnel on the more mundane parts of the project. Again, we ask the client who can be spared to work with us, and usually discover that one of the reasons the client wants to use consultants in the first place is lack of manpower.

Our final tactic is to give a percentage discount after a set number of days' work – usually ten days. Most of our projects are under ten days anyway so we give very little, but the client feels he has gained.

Fees for associates
This is simple for us – we give 33 per cent of what we charge the client. If you give less, either you get associates who are not up to the job or who are so demotivated they perform badly or try and steal the client from you. However, make sure you get your associates to sign that they take responsibility for their own tax for you are liable until they do (see the recommended tax form we use for associates in Appendices).

In our work, about 45 per cent of fees are on a project basis, 35 per cent on a per day basis, and the remainder a mixture of the two. We have yet to be asked to work to a performance contract where you are paid on results. We once completed an Absentee Management programme and have regretted ever since that we did not charge the client a percentage of identified savings.

Collecting your fees
The advice here is easy – as soon as possible. If you don't put in an invoice quickly clients will not pay you

quickly. Also clients have short memories about how effective your service was. Views about your work go something like this:

Week 1 That was a great project/programme
Week 2 That was a good project/programme
Week 3 The project/programme was OK
Week 4 Couldn't we have done that for ourselves?
Week 5 Was it really worth doing in the first place?
Week 6 I think we are being over-charged
Week 7 Why did we ever use a consultancy in the first place?

Invoice early while satisfaction is still warm.

Many firms will maximize their cash flow at the expense of yours. We have found that the larger or more blue-chip the firm, the longer they take to pay. However, most are sympathetic to the idea that you are a small consultancy. If asking them to make an exception in your case doesn't work, negotiate a premium for any delay in payment over 30 days. As a last resort, when you are invited to work again for a bad-paying client, build in a contingency for late payment in your fee structure. This has been a real benefit for us. We have one client who is such a bad payer we ask for 'cash with enquiry'.

KEEPING YOUR CLIENTS

You clients list is like a garden, you must tend it regularly. Existing clients will always provide you with more work than new clients. Also, they will be the source of new clients through referrals.

When you consider that it might take you five or six days of visits, planning and presentations over a six-month period before you gain a new client, they are very valuable indeed. Once a consultancy is accepted by a client, unless some really poor work is done, it is surprising how loyal they are. We have worked with one hospital group for over 15 years. It is not that they have given us much work – about seven days per year in fact – but even so that represents 105 days work, which is larger than any contract we have ever had with any client in any *one* year.

One thing has surprised us, and that is how often clients box you in so that they think of you as only providing one type of service or product. At one time our consultancy did mainly industrial relations work before branching out into general skills training and then outplacement. We worked with one firm every year providing negotiation training with their executive team as a precursor to their annual face-to-face dance around the wage pole with their unions. One year we were amazed and ashamed of ourselves to discover that they had closed a unit and used another consultancy for the provision of outplacement, an area in which by then we had more expertise than in negotiation training. We had lost the opportunity because we had not kept the client informed. So this brings us to the next point.

Updating clients

It is unlikely that clients are going to give you significantly long projects on a regular basis. If there were such projects the client would soon work out that it would be better and cheaper to have its own internal consultancy team, or hire some people on short-term contracts. So, if you are not going to be in 'the mind's eye' of your clients you must update them just to remind them who you are and what you are doing. Let your clients enjoy your successes by sharing them with you. There are a variety of ways of doing this, some involving more work than others. The most difficult is the newsletter, because once you start you have to keep going, and it is surprising, when you are small, how much news you don't have and how rapacious a news-letter is for items that will of interest to clients. If you are not careful the news becomes very self-congrat-ulatory and bumptious. Writing articles which are well-researched, interesting and of direct use to clients is a good way of keeping in contact with them. These have the added benefit of being occasional papers rather than having to be pushed out like the newsletters on a regular basis. Where appropriate, clients can be invited to make contributions. It always generates a warm feeling to see yourself in print.

One of us sends out a 'puff' letter regularly. This is just a single side of A4 with new clients, projects worked on, media appearances and publications, and any other points of general interest about the consultancy. It is rather like a synopsis of a newsletter and clients tell us they find them interesting.

Writing articles for journals and newspapers is not only a good way of promoting the consultancy – writing always gives you a larger shadow than you deserve – you can then send them to your clients. Clients like to know that their consultants are doing well and that they have hired people whose views and ideas are worthy of publication.

If you publish a book, get your publisher to run off 300 extra book covers. These make wonderful contact mat-erial. You can write a personal note on the back, to-gether with the publication date. At a stroke you stay in contact with your client and promote your book at the same time.

Keeping up with the buying chain
Organizations are not static because the people in them are on the move all the time – either being promoted within the organization or promoting themselves out of

the organization. It is essential that you stay in touch with the buying chain for this very reason. You will find that, unless you are careful, your relationship is with just one person in the organization and once that person leaves or is promoted then your relationship with the client dies. If you can manage the process effectively you can keep the old client by introducing yourself quickly to the new incumbent and just as quickly following the original incumbent, thus gaining a new client. It is like new lamps for old, without losing the old. With one client we have worked with no fewer than seven different Training Managers and/or training specialists and we have five new clients, because, when they left we were taken with them. It is as if they were on our marketing team.

CLIENT LOYALTY

Make a point of using your clients' products. Reciprocal loyalty is expected. Woe betide you if you drive into Goodyear with Michelin tyres, or take notes at Parker Pen with a Waterman.

We shop at Safeway, eat Uncle Sam's hamburgers, drive on Goodyear tyres and this book is written with a Parker pen, before being put on to a SUN work station. We bank at Barclays and are insured by Laurentian. We have some problem with atomic weapons, but we pay our taxes on time since we consult with the Inland Revenue and Customs & Excise. Customs & Excise, we know from experience, check on your VAT status before confirming an assignment.

Using clients' products helps you get closer to them, understand their problems and identify potential consultancy opportunities. You can also make sensible conversation with them since you are a user.

The next best thing, once you get going, is to buy

shares in the company. I don't live in a Bovis house, but I have some P&O shares, nor do I wear Marks & Spencer suits, but my shareholding ensures that I get the Company Report.

Be loyal to your customers and they are more likely to be loyal to you.

REDUCING THE OVERHEADS

Most consultancies fail for just three reasons and none of them are to do with the product or service. They fail because of marketing failure, lack of financial management and high overheads. Let's have a look at overheads.

A colleague of ours, when he first set up his consultancy:

Hired expensive offices
Engaged a secretary
Leased an expensive car
Bought expensive office furniture

and went out of business in six months having lost almost all his golden handshake from the firm which made him redundant.

THE CAR

Cars are difficult, mainly because of the peculiar place they hold in western culture as a status item. In the trade they are called 'badge-brands' because they not only indicate status but also project an image with an emotional value – you are represented by the car you drive.

If the car is too old, unless it is a classic with a cherished number plate, then the consultancy cannot be doing too well and there are doubts about your lasting the duration of the contract. If the car is new and expensive, then obviously you are ripping your client off and charging too much. We know one consultant who drives a Ferrari, charges top rates and wants to get out of the business but this is the exception.

Think of the image your consultancy has in your client's mind and think which car could best project that image.

If you are starting up and you have no choice but to use your faithful banger then use it, but park close to the client's nearest taxi rank and do the last lap by taxi. Don't park round the corner because clients frequently walk you to reception to see you out, especially if it has been a good meeting and/or they want a private word. For the same reason, keep your car clean and tidy inside and out. Consultants tend to use their cars as offices and, after a week on the road, your car can be the pits. One of us had the embarrassment of driving the client round his establishment, a large government organization, to get to his office whilst the car was littered with personal items. In the same vein, cigarette butts and crisp papers in the ashtray somehow does not do much for a professional image.

Nor is it just the car. One of us has Goodyear tyres, not only because they are excellent but Goodyear is a client. I once had to get into Ford HQ in Essex driving my Volvo. Not only did they not let me get into the car park, I did not get the business either.

If you have an old car, keep it in good condition and think about an expensive personalized plate – preferably using your firm's initials – and then the age cannot be easily guessed.

And finally . . .

This book has been designed to help you achieve success in consultancy. Many thousands of consultants all over the world are making a very healthy living from passing on the benefits of their knowledge and ideas to others. They are loving every minute of it and getting paid handsomely. Here's to your consultancy! Be bold and be true to yourself and go for gold!

Oh, and . . .

'If you obey all the rules you miss all the fun!
Katherine Hepburn

APPENDICES

1. **Information about consultants**
   Obtainable from:
   Management Consultancies Association
   Institute of Management Consultants
   Specialist Organizations e.g. IPD
   Management Consultancy Information Service
   Government Departments and public organizations
   sometimes advertise, inviting interest.

2. **Information about businesses**
   Kompass Volume III (30,000 employees)
   Kompass Regional Guide
   Dun and Bradstreet
   Personnel Managers Yearbook
   The Hambro Company Guide
   Key British Enterprises – several volumes of
   Britain's top 50,000 companies
   Business Pages (Red, similar to Yellow Pages but
   devoted to businesses)
   The Times 1000 – Leading Companies
   Jordan's Best of British – the top 20,000 companies
   Extell Quoted Companies
   Trade Association and Professional Bodies of the
   UK, Pergamon Press
   Croner's A–Z of Business Information Services
   Yellow Pages

3. A sample proposal

PROPOSAL FOR THE DELIVERY OF TRAINING IN STRESS MANAGEMENT TO MANAGERS

To
HEALTHPACK FOODS LTD

Prepared for	**Prepared by**
Albert Norris	Barbara Greyshott
Managing Director	Senior Consultant
Healthpack Foods Ltd	John Green Associates
Grimsby Street	Perry Street
Hull	Leeds

June 19XX

BACKGROUND

Healthpack Foods Ltd has successfully ridden the recession and has increased its market sector in the sales of pre-packaged ready meals.

Whilst the market appeal has increased, Healthpack Foods Ltd has slimmed down its workforce to ensure economic viability and competitiveness. The company recognizes that its staff, its most valuable asset, is coping with a greater workload with fewer staff than before. In addition, it recognizes that staff bring problems to work with them, which affect their well-being and their ability to function on the job. Healthpack Foods is anxious to ensure that its managers initially, and then progressively all its staff, learn to recognize the symptoms of stress in themselves and their work colleagues and to build the resources to combat these inevitable stresses.

Healthpack Foods is proud of its reputation for promoting health. It is keen to show its commitment to its staff in a programme of Stress Awareness Seminars and Stress Management Workshops. Commencement of the training will accompany quality initiatives which will signal a culture change in the company. The total package is expected to enhance the viability of the company and increase the well-being and commitment of its employees.

PROGRAMME OVERVIEW

John Green Associates is able to offer a customized range of support to clients experiencing the effects of organizational change.

The Benefits

Improved personal effectiveness
Increased productivity
Support for key personnel
Reduced levels of absenteeism
Cost savings

THE PROGRAMME

1. Stress Awareness Seminars

For the busy executive who requires an initial introduction to the subject of stress, this seminar is designed to be a catalyst for action in the company. Gaining the commitment of the top executives in the company is the all-important indicator of success and this seminar will provide an opportunity to focus on the stresses in the organization and some of the remedies which can be applied.

They incorporate:
> European legislation and its implications for employers
> Definition of stress
> Its causes and effects
> Symptoms in the workplace
> Remedies and Coping Strategies – an introduction

Methods:
> The Seminars are highly interactive, with group exercises and discussion focusing on topics of particular relevance to Healthpack Foods. An informal facilitation approach is adopted to maximize benefits to participants.

Length of seminar: Half-day
Seminar size: Up to 15 participants
Number of Trainers: One

2. Stress Management Workshops

These workshops provide an opportunity for managers and staff to explore in more depth what stress is and to focus on its effects on the individual, the group and the workplace.

They incorporate:
    Consideration of current legal issues
    Benefits of stress management in the workplace
    Definition of stress
    Individual differences/perceptions
    Causes and effects of stress
    Personality factors
    Coping strategies:
        cognitive approaches
        relaxation techniques
        time management
        lifestyle management
    Personal stress contract

Methods:
    The one- and two-day workshops provide an
    opportunity for participants to examine stresses in
    the workplace through a mixture of pair and triad
    work, group discussion, practical exercises and in-
    dividual learning. A video will be shown which will
    form the basis of a focused company comparison.

Length of workshops: One or two days
Workshop size: 8-10 participants
Number of trainers: One or two, depending on length
of workshop

Each participant will receive the uniquely predictive
JGA Stress Assessment Guide before and after the training to measure the effectiveness of the workshop ses-
sions.

Fees

Prices applicable from 1 October 19XX to 31 September 19XX

	Per unit
1. Stress Awareness Seminars	£x00
2. Stress Management Workshops – One day	£y000
– Two day	£z000

3. JGA Stress Assessment Guide – to include pre- and post-workshop assessment

These fees are exclusive of VAT at the current rate and receipted direct out of pocket expenses at cost.

Successful projects undertaken so far

John Green Associates have recently completed a pilot programme of Stress Management Training for all managers and staff in the North Eastern Area of the Headway Group of Supermarkets. Six months later, and following a further programme of Counselling Skills Training, the sickness and absenteeism levels in the North Eastern Area have reduced by 1.5 per cent and 2 per cent respectively. The programme is now being extended to the remainder of the UK.

Following a successful programme of Stress Management Workshops in Leigh Health Authority, we have now been invited to 'Train the Trainers', key personnel in five hospitals, to cascade Stress Awareness programmes to front-line staff.

4. A sample mailshot letter

Ms J Fergus
Chief Executive
Cranbourne Chemicals Ltd
Weybridge Street
GLOUCESTER

Dear Ms Fergus

CAREER ORIENTATION – THE KEY TO GREATER EFFECTIVENESS

We understand that Cranbourne Chemicals has recently undergone a major staffing reductions programme together with a move to new premises. Could I ask you to spare a couple of minutes to consider whether we might help you?

Our recent experience shows us that many recently reorganized companies, like your own, are now helping their employees to reassess their career goals. The benefits come from increased productivity and the releasing of untapped potential.

The **Westgate** Career Orientation Service gives a new sense of purpose and direction to staff who may be recovering from the effects of reductions programmes.

Application:
    Change in career direction
    Re-organization and re-engineering of departments
    Re-motivating stayers
    Re-orientating square pegs in round holes

Benefits:
    Smoother pathway to change
    More effective team working
    Greater personal effectiveness
    Improved morale
    Enhanced productivity
    Caring company image

Our Career Orientation Programmes have recently been implemented in the Midlands Health Group, where we have ...., in Pimlico Pharmaceuticals, where ...., and in Trubshaw & Sons (Construction), who retained our services to .... All of these organizations will be pleased to talk to you about the professionalism of our approach and the effectiveness of our results.

I enclose a brochure which outlines the full range of our services and I would be delighted to visit you and explain these in more detail. I will ring you in the next few days to establish whether this would be of interest to you. I shall, in any case, be in your area on Wednesday, 22nd of the month.

Yours sincerely,
Westgate Associates

Paul Duffy

5. Essential equipment/services
An office (a dedicated room at home will suffice)
Desk
Telephone
Ansaphone
Fax Machine
PC and Printer
Business Software
Business Stationery Business Cards
                                   Letterhead
                                   Compliment Slips
                                   Leaflet or Brochure
Four-drawer filing cabinet with hanging files
Access to typing services
Professional journals

Desirable – if you can afford them
Answering service/Paging service
Mobile telephone
Secretary
Office premises

People you'll need to contact when setting up your business
Inland Revenue
VAT – HM Customs and Excise
Department of Social Security – National Insurance Contributions
An accountant
Bank
Professional indemnity/public liability insurers
Pensions advisor

6. A 'Keeping in Touch' Letter

Dear Mark

MANAGING THE CHANGE PROCESS
It was a pleasure to visit you and Alistair Gillmore at Craven Brothers yesterday, to find out more about your current needs/to make my presentation on 'Building for the Future'/to finalize the arrangements for the Staff Survey.

I was particularly interested to learn more about the company's future plans for expanding its research facilities, and I am confident that we will increase Craven's commercial success and competitiveness through this very exciting project. It occurred to me on the way back to the office that another very positive outcome of our working together would be that you could use the results of the current work to set up the new laboratories in the most efficient and cost-effective way.

I know you will need some time to consider our discussions and to talk them over with your Board. I will telephone you early next week to see if there are any further issues I can help you with.

Yours sincerely,
STIRLING ASSOCIATES

CHRIS STIRLING
Managing Director

7. Client numbering systems

There are only two reasons we can think of for using a numbering system. One is to help with paperwork, and the other is to show the client that you are a substantial consultancy of standing, having been in business ages, and that you have stacks of clients.

When we started we were given the usual advice of starting our invoicing at 500 so that early clients did not realize they were part of our experimentation – would you like to be the first operation for a newly qualified surgeon? We tried it, but after a year or we swapped it to the following:

Client No./Financial Year/Invoice Number for that year

Thus, 212/97/34 means nothing to the clients but to us it means the 34th invoice in the financial year 1997 for client 212, who happens to be Customs and Excise. It helps us to know how many clients we have and also how much work we have in any one year with that client and the consultancy. No doubt you will develop your own system, but it has to be better than just a single number.

8. A sample invoice

Janet Dale Associates
42 High Street
Leeds
LS2 6JG

INVOICE

Mr Alex Fraser
Regional Director
Starlight International
Burymead Buildings
Manchester M2 1ND

Invoice No: 126/95/263
Invoice Date: 21 November 19XX

Description	Amount £
To: Provision of 2-day Team-building Workshop 12 & 13 November 19XX	1000.00
Expenses (see attached breakdown)	242.00
Subtotal	1242.00
VAT @ 17.5%	217.00
TOTAL	1459.35

Terms of Business: 14 days

VAT No. 623228756

9. Client contact form

Name:	
Address:	
Tel/Fax:	
Type of business:	

Source of contact Cold call ☐ Network ☐
Referral ☐ Advert ☐
Other ☐

Main contact:	Tel:
Contact 2:	Tel:
Contact 3:	Tel:

Main areas of interest in consultancy:

Dates of meetings:	Summary of outcomes:

Company culture/Impressions:

Suggested fee structure:

Actions required:

10. Tax form for associates

NAME OF ASSOCIATE: DATE:

TRADING NAME:

BUSINESS ADDRESS:

VAT NO. :

I certify that:

a) All fees and other income received by me (or my company) from Transcareer Consulting Group are declared by me (or my company) to the Inland Revenue;

b) My Schedule D tax reference number is .... and my accounts are submitted to HM Inspector of Taxes.
   .... District;

c) I (we) accept full responsibility for any liability to tax and/or National Insurance Contributions arising in respect of all payments received from Transcareer Consulting Group;

d) I do/do not pay Class 2 and Class 4 National Insurance contributions;

e) I accept that in the absence of the above information tax and NIC may be withheld from all payments (except for reimbursement of actual expenses) made to me (or my company) by Transcareer Consulting Group.

Signed: _____ Date:_____

Many readers write to ask if Max and Elaine are available for consultancy assignments. The answer, of course, is yes and we can be contacted at the following addresses:

Max A Eggert
Transcareer
94 High Street
Lindfield
West Sussex RH16 2HP
Tel: 0144448 3057

Elaine van der Zeil
2 The Meade
Wilmslow
Cheshire SK9 2JF
Tel: 01625 535090

Both of us work separately and in collaboration in the areas of Career Management, Outplacement, Human Resource Management and Stress Management.

Feedback on this, or indeed any of our publications, is always welcome.